SMP 16–19

Statistics

Foundations of sampling and estimation

CAMBRIDGE
UNIVERSITY PRESS

Much of this book is based on earlier SMP books to which the following people contributed.

Chris Belsom
Stan Dolan
Judith Galsworthy
Andy Hall
Mike Hall
Janet Jagger
Ann Kitchen
Melissa Rodd

Paul Roder
Tom Roper
Mike Savage
Bernard Taylor
Carole Tyler
Nigel Webb
Julian Williams
Phil Wood

PUBLISHED BY THE PRESS SYNDICATE OF THE UNIVERSITY OF CAMBRIDGE
The Pitt Building, Trumpington Street, Cambridge, United Kingdom

CAMBRIDGE UNIVERSITY PRESS
The Edinburgh Building, Cambridge, CB2 2RU, UK
40 West 20th Street, New York, NY 10011–4211, USA
10 Stamford Road, Oakleigh, VIC 3166, Australia
Ruiz de Alarcón 13, 28014 Madrid, Spain
Dock House, The Waterfront, Cape Town 8001, South Africa

http://www.cambridge.org

First published 2001

Printed in the United Kingdom at the University Press, Cambridge

Typeface Minion and Officina   System QuarkXpress®

A catalogue record for this book is available from the British Library

ISBN 0 521 78802 1 paperback

Acknowledgements

The authors and publishers would like to thank the following for supplying photographs:

page 48   © Hulton–Deutsch Collection/CORBIS (market research); © Tony Stone Images/Terry Vine
(lab technician)

page 51   © CORBIS

Cover photograph: © Tony Stone Images/Art Wolfe

Contents

Using this book

Most sections within a chapter consist of work developing new ideas followed by an exercise for practice in using those ideas.

Within the development sections, some questions and activities are labelled with a **D**, for example **2D**, and are enclosed in a box. These involve issues that are worth exploring through discussion – either teacher-led discussion in the whole class or discussion by students in small groups, who may then feed back their conclusions to the whole class.

Questions labelled **E** are more demanding.

In several places the use of computer simulations of the behaviour of various populations is recommended.

Particularly effective is the DISCUS package of helpfully interactive Excel-based programs, downloadable from www.mis.coventry.ac.uk/research/discus/discus_home.html

A more recent version, DISCUSS, can be found at heracles.coventry.ac.uk/volume

DISCUSS was not complete in time for detailed references to be given in the text of this book.

For current information on the availability of these packages, go to the SMP's site, www.smpmaths.org.uk

Simulations can also be carried out using Autograph, which is available from Eastmond Publishing Ltd, PO Box 46, Oundle, PE8 4JX, www.autograph-math.com

1 The binomial distribution

A Probability and Pascal's triangle (answers p. 103)

This is a binostat. It is like a pinball machine; balls are
fed in at the top, fall through a triangular grid and collect
in a series of slots. The picture shows the distribution
in the slots after a number of balls have passed through
the grid.

1D | The picture shows that more balls collect in the central slots than
in the outside slots. Why do you think this happens?

To examine what is going on in more detail, consider the following
simple binostat.

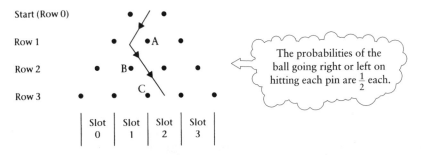

The probabilities of the
ball going right or left on
hitting each pin are $\frac{1}{2}$ each.

The rows and slots have been labelled for reference. You will see later
that it is helpful to label the slots starting with 0 rather than 1.

The arrow shows *one* possible route for a ball which ends up in slot 2.
The ball hits the pin at A and goes through the gap on the left (as you
look at the diagram). At B it hits the pin and goes through the gap on
the right; at C it goes right again, ending up in slot number 2.

2 Find how many different routes the ball could take to slot 2. What is
the probability of each route? Deduce the probability of a ball falling
into slot 2.

3 Repeat the calculation of question 1 for slots 0, 1 and 3, and hence
write down the probability distribution of the random variable X,
where X = slot number.

4 Use the result of question 3 to predict the expected frequencies of balls
landing in each slot when 400 balls are used.

5 This is a binostat with two rows. By considering the number of routes to slots 0, 1 and 2, find the probability distribution of X = slot number.

Calculate the expected number of balls in each slot when 400 balls are used.

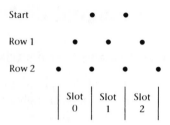

For a larger number of rows, you need a way of calculating the number of routes to each slot. Consider this binostat with four rows.

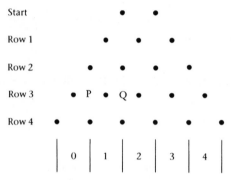

6 Find the probability of taking any particular route through this binostat.

To find how many routes there are to, for example, slot 1, you can use the fact that all routes to this slot pass through *either* P *or* Q (see diagram).

7 By writing down the number of routes to points P and Q, deduce how many routes there are to slot 1 and hence the probability of a ball falling into this slot.

8 Repeat the argument for the other slots and hence write down the probability distribution for X = slot number in this case.

The results obtained above can be summarised as follows.

- The number of routes to each position or slot is given by the following triangle, where each number is the sum of the numbers in the previous row immediately to the left and to the right.

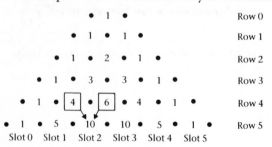

- For a binostat with n rows (not counting the first row of pins), there are 2^n equally likely paths and the probability of a ball following one particular path is $\dfrac{1}{2^n}$.

You can use the results above to find the probability distribution for a ball's final position.

You may already recognise this triangle of numbers from previous work. It is known as **Pascal's triangle**, after the French mathematician Blaise Pascal (1623–1663).

The sort of probability distribution you found for the binostat occurs quite often. Before thinking about the circumstances in which it arises, you will need a generalised interpretation of the numbers in Pascal's triangle.

Consider this three-row binostat.

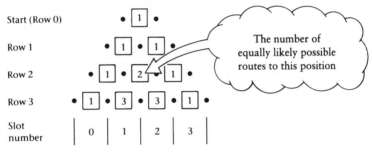

Notice that the 'slot number' just gives the number of times the ball is deflected to the right in its path to the slot. So, for example, to get to slot 2, the ball must be deflected twice to the right (and hence once to the left) out of the total of three deflections. So the number of routes to slot 2 is simply the number of ways of choosing two deflections out of three to be 'right', namely L R R, R L R and R R L.

Similarly, the entry '10' in slot 2 of row 5 on p. 2 gives the number of ways of choosing 2 'right' deflections out of 5. It could equally give the number of ways of getting 2 heads from 5 tosses, or choosing 2 presents from 5 presents, or more generally choosing 2 things from 5.

This number is written as $\dbinom{5}{2}$. You can now use Pascal's triangle to work out similar probability distributions.

Example 1

A coin is tossed. Find the number of ways, and hence the probability, of getting these.

(a) Exactly two heads from three tosses

(b) Exactly two tails from six tosses

Solution

(a) There are $\binom{3}{2} = 3$ ways of choosing two heads from three tosses,

namely HHT, HTH and THH. As there is a total of eight (2^3) possible outcomes, the probability is

$$P(2 \text{ heads}) = 3 \times \frac{1}{2^3} = \frac{3}{8}.$$

(b) Six tosses have $2^6 = 64$ possible equally likely outcomes.

Two tails can occur $\binom{6}{2}$ ways, which are obtained as row 6, slot 2 of the triangle.

			Slot 2				
Row 6	1	6	(15)	20	15	6	1

$$\Rightarrow \binom{6}{2} = 15$$

$$\Rightarrow P (2 \text{ tails}) = 15 \times \tfrac{1}{64} = \tfrac{15}{64}$$

9D You can find values like $\binom{7}{5}$ quickly using tables or a calculator.

Find out about one of these methods.

Exercise A (answers p. 103)

1 Extend the triangle as necessary to work out these.

(a) The number of ways of choosing 4 objects from 7 objects

(b) $\binom{7}{5}$ (c) $\binom{6}{4}$ (d) $\binom{5}{2}$ (e) $\binom{2}{1}$

(f) $\binom{7}{3}$ (g) $\binom{5}{4}$ (h) $\binom{5}{5}$

2 A coin is tossed 7 times. In how many ways can you get these results exactly?

(a) 2 heads   (b) 5 tails

Explain your answers. What does this tell you about Pascal's triangle?

3 A pack of playing cards (without jokers) is cut eight times. What is the probability of cutting a red card on exactly six occasions?

4 Assuming that boy and girl births are equally likely, what is the probability that a family of four children will contain three or more girls?

5 In a nuclear reaction, a free neutron has an equal chance of being absorbed or colliding to produce a fission. What is the probability that out of five free neutrons each of these events will occur?

(a) All will be absorbed.
(b) All but two will be absorbed.

6 A bag contains equal numbers of white and red marbles. Ten players in turn draw a marble from the bag and replace it. What is the probability that precisely five players draw a white marble?

B The binomial probability model (answers p. 103)

So far, you have modelled the probabilities for repetitions (or trials) of an event with two possible outcomes (for example head or tail, boy or girl, etc. ...) which are assumed to be equally likely to occur. You have found that the probability of r outcomes from n trials is

number of choices of r from $n \times$ probability of each choice

$$= \binom{n}{r} \times \frac{1}{2^n}$$

What if the two outcomes are not equally likely?

This is equivalent to a binostat which is not properly balanced, so the probability of deflecting to the left is greater than to the right. The distribution of balls in the slots becomes 'skewed': there are more balls in the left-hand slots than the right.

1 A binostat with three rows is tilted so that for each deflection there is a probability of 0.6 of the ball going left (and hence 0.4 of going right).

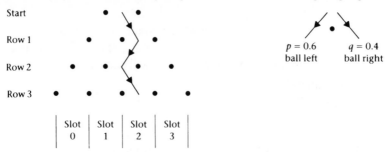

(a) Calculate the probability of a ball taking the route shown above to slot 2. What assumption are you making when you multiply the probabilities for each deflection?

(b) Calculate the probability of a ball falling into slot 2 by any other route.

(c) Calculate the probability of a ball falling into slot 2.

(d) Repeat the calculation for slots 0, 1 and 3 and hence find the probability distribution of $X =$ slot number.

(e) Calculate the expected frequencies if 500 balls are sent down this binostat.

(f) Calculate the probability distribution for 5 rows, with $p = 0.6$ as before.

(g) Calculate the probability distribution for X with $p = 0.2$ and 3 rows.

You can now generalise the probability model to all situations when:

- there are n repetitions or trials of an event, the outcomes of which are *independent*
- the value of n is fixed
- the probability of a particular outcome is fixed
- you are counting the number of times this outcome occurs.

The probability distribution for the random variable R is found by:

(a) working out the probability of a sequence containing r occurrences out of n

(b) then multiplying by the number of ways of getting this outcome, namely $\binom{n}{r}$.

Probability models of this type are called **binomial** probability models.

Example 2

Three fair dice are thrown. What is the probability of throwing two sixes?

Solution

The probability of, for example, (six) (no six) (six)

is $\dfrac{1}{6} \times \dfrac{5}{6} \times \dfrac{1}{6}$

So the probability of two sixes is $\dbinom{3}{2} \times \dfrac{1}{6} \times \dfrac{5}{6} \times \dfrac{1}{6}$

$$= 3 \times \dfrac{1}{6} \times \dfrac{5}{6} \times \dfrac{1}{6} = \dfrac{5}{72}$$

Example 3

On average 90% of seeds from a particular packet germinate. If you plant ten seeds in a row, what is the probability of eight or more germinating?

Solution

The probability of, say, the first eight germinating and the last two dying is

$$0.9 \times 0.9 \times \ldots \times 0.9 \times 0.1 \times 0.1 = (0.9)^8 (0.1)^2.$$

Extending Pascal's triangle to row 10 shows that the number of ways of getting exactly eight germinations is

$$\binom{10}{8} = 45.$$

So the probability of eight germinations is

$$45 \times (0.9)^8 (0.1)^2 = 0.1937 \qquad \text{(to 4 s.f.)}$$

Similarly, the probability of nine germinations is

$$10 \times (0.9)^9 \times 0.1 = 0.3874 \qquad \text{(to 4 s.f.)}$$

and of all ten germinating is

$$1 \times (0.9)^{10} = 0.3487 \qquad \text{(to 4 s.f.)}$$

So the total probability of eight or more is

$$0.1937 + 0.3874 + 0.3487 = 0.93 \qquad \text{(to 2 s.f.)}$$

The binomial probability distribution can be summarised as follows.

> Given n trials of an event, the probability of r occurrences of an outcome which has a probability p of occurring at each trial is
>
> $$\binom{n}{r} p^r (1-p)^{n-r}$$
>
> assuming that the trials are independent.

2D 'When a piece of toast drops to the floor, it usually lands buttered-side down.'

(Murphy's law)

(a) Does the evidence in the cartoon prove Murphy's law?

(b) Would Murphy's law be proved if 70 out of 100 pieces landed buttered-side down?

On the assumption that the outcomes of 'butter up' and 'butter down' are equally likely, the probability of seven slices out of ten landing 'butter down' is

$$\binom{10}{7}(0.5)^7(0.5)^3 = 0.117.$$

The full probability distribution for the random variable R, the 'number of "butter down" slices out of ten' is given below.

r	0	1	2	3	4	5	6	7	8	9	10
$P(R=r)$	0.001	0.010	0.044	0.117	0.205	0.246	0.205	0.117	0.044	0.010	0.001

$$P(R = r) = \binom{10}{r} 0.5^r \, 0.5^{10-r}$$

Notice that no single result in itself has a high probability.

No matter what the probability is for a single slice landing 'butter down', getting *exactly* seven slices out of ten 'butter down' will have a fairly low probability, and so considering the probability of this event does not help to decide about Murphy's law.

The probability of an event such as 'seven *or more* butter-side down' is a much more discriminating test of the proposed model and so you should always consider the probability of such events when testing a model, rather than P(seven exactly).

From the table the probability of seven or more slices landing butter-side down is $0.117 + 0.044 + 0.010 + 0.001 = 0.172$.

So, assuming that Murphy's law is incorrect and that 'butter up' and 'butter down' are equally likely, you can expect a result of seven or more 'butter down' slices out of ten on about one in six occasions. This is quite often, and so the result is not very significant evidence in favour of Murphy's law.

Calculating the likelihood of getting 70 or more out of 100 'butter down', given an equal chance of landing either way, is explored in Chapter 5. The probability of this result is about 0.001, so observing such an event *would* be strong evidence in support of Murphy's law.

Exercise B (answers p. 104)

1 Four dice are thrown. Calculate the probability distribution for S, the number of sixes thrown.

2 'Eight out of ten prefer Wizzo to Wow' is the sort of claim advertisements sometimes make. It could be based on one sample of only ten people!

   (a) Assume that Wizzo is no better or worse than Wow. Work out the probability that out of a random sample of ten people who were offered the choice, eight or more prefer Wizzo to Wow.

   (b) Assume Wizzo is in fact preferred by 80% of people. Work out the probability that out of a random sample of ten people, eight or more prefer Wizzo to Wow.

3 Birth statistics show that 51% of babies born in Britain are male. Use this to calculate the probability that a family of four children will contain three or more girls.

4 Oxford vs. Cambridge Boat Race statistics to date show that Oxford has won on 54% of occasions. Use a binomial model to calculate the probability that Cambridge wins three times in a period of five years. Do you think the model is appropriate in this case? Explain.

5 (a) Poker dice have six faces marked ace, king, queen, jack, 10 and 9. What is the probability of throwing three or more aces with five dice?

(b) A player gets three or more aces three times out of four throws. Calculate the probability of this event.

6 A cricket captain wins the toss nine times out of ten. Investigate how lucky this is.

7 Weather statistics for Blackpool in July indicate that it rains one day in three. The Wilsons take a week's holiday there in July, and it rains on six days out of seven. Use a binomial model to estimate how unlucky this is. Is the model appropriate?

8 In a test of a new recipe for a popular soft drink, eight people sampled a glass of new and a glass of original. Out of these, seven preferred the new flavour, and one the original. How strong is this evidence that the new recipe is in fact better?

9 A rare plant is difficult to grow. Each seed has a 20% chance of germinating.

(a) If I plant five seeds, what chance is there that at least one will germinate?

(b) Investigate a how many seeds I should plant to get a 90% chance of at least one germination.

C Sampling (answers p. 105)

The illustration demonstrates these examples of sampling:

- taking a 'taster' from a vat of wine
- road testing a vehicle, perhaps to assess its safety in a collision
- surveying opinions by questioning – market research perhaps.

A central problem of statistics is how to use information from a **sample** to infer whatever one can about the **parent population** from which the sample is taken.

1D | By considering the examples on the previous page and some of your own, think of various reasons why you might want to use a sample rather than test every member of the population.

What makes for a 'good' sample?

When attempting to draw conclusions on the basis of a particular sample it is vital to consider whether the method of selecting the sample is likely to have introduced bias.

To enable reliable information to be obtained about a population from a sample, it is important to be careful about *how* the sample is chosen.

On the next page are the heights in centimetres of 300 sixth-formers. The data have been listed so that each row of ten figures across the page consists of five boys' heights followed by the heights of five girls.

2D | Take samples from the heights of 300 sixth-formers given on page 12 in order to estimate the mean height for the group. Use two different **sampling procedures**:

A Start anywhere on the page and select the next five numbers in that column.

B Start anywhere on the page and select the next five numbers across the page.

Although the heights listed form a fairly small group, this is an example of a *population* from which *samples* can be selected.

Collect the results from your whole class so that you obtain a distribution of sample means for sampling procedure A and another for sampling procedure B. (At least fifty results from each procedure are necessary.) Record your results in a systematic way.

The population mean height for the entire group of 300 sixth-formers is actually 167.4 cm.

(a) How close were your sample estimates?
How close were the estimates produced by the rest of the class?
Which procedure gave the better results?

(b) What criticisms do you have of the sampling procedures used in this experiment?
How could they be improved?

170.1	172.2	179.3	176.4	168.9	168.1	154.8	157.0	164.8	165.3
178.1	181.1	180.4	178.3	179.6	160.3	157.7	151.5	157.0	159.3
176.6	175.0	170.5	181.2	168.5	158.6	153.0	155.5	170.5	159.4
178.8	172.4	163.6	167.0	176.3	155.4	157.4	160.4	165.7	161.2
173.3	179.4	177.9	165.2	172.5	157.3	164.1	160.7	160.1	156.3
175.3	186.1	176.6	169.6	174.1	164.4	153.8	160.2	163.0	157.6
165.9	162.7	166.2	168.7	163.7	168.8	154.6	173.8	155.3	159.9
171.4	170.0	181.5	181.0	176.6	158.7	168.3	159.8	154.9	155.7
184.3	175.1	188.0	181.4	171.7	167.1	150.5	152.9	165.3	154.2
175.9	173.0	173.0	175.0	178.1	159.5	160.3	160.9	179.6	167.3
175.0	162.8	178.4	163.7	163.7	162.9	175.6	165.4	165.6	162.1
169.0	163.6	167.9	164.9	181.9	155.7	152.0	141.1	152.0	168.8
167.1	174.1	172.0	180.1	176.7	150.2	164.6	158.3	156.2	170.1
159.9	160.2	173.7	173.7	169.4	157.0	156.9	166.2	156.8	163.2
168.5	170.0	176.3	166.2	163.4	164.2	171.2	164.1	168.3	160.0
167.8	171.0	179.9	177.2	183.8	169.3	166.3	162.5	168.9	153.2
179.7	167.4	172.7	175.8	168.7	162.3	172.3	171.9	159.1	164.7
179.0	177.6	160.8	186.7	182.3	155.9	166.0	162.8	163.8	157.4
171.3	162.2	173.3	170.0	184.9	157.0	155.0	171.8	164.8	162.5
165.2	173.1	180.2	175.1	168.8	161.1	159.4	159.2	162.2	156.7
178.2	171.8	175.2	178.0	173.9	171.8	166.0	166.9	162.7	157.2
163.7	189.1	175.1	171.0	171.1	156.2	166.5	164.4	154.7	156.3
182.6	173.7	168.8	183.3	170.3	164.7	162.3	175.7	160.0	176.4
167.9	179.4	171.2	170.6	175.5	172.9	156.6	162.9	153.7	160.8
171.0	174.8	176.1	172.9	170.5	167.3	146.4	164.5	159.1	170.4
174.8	178.4	180.9	177.2	163.3	150.4	157.3	168.3	156.8	169.4
170.6	185.9	173.2	179.5	179.7	163.6	155.1	152.9	166.7	156.8
175.6	172.2	178.9	164.9	172.0	153.7	166.7	160.0	163.7	158.9
178.8	182.0	160.5	183.6	163.6	150.3	179.3	158.0	161.5	164.6
172.3	169.6	182.9	168.2	159.9	161.7	153.9	158.5	165.5	161.1

An important requirement of a sample is that every member of the population has an equal chance of being selected. The sample members must be selected at **random**.

3 In each of the following examples, decide what bias, if any, the sampling procedure has introduced.

(a) To obtain information about diseases amongst the elderly, everyone in a large residential home is given a thorough health check.

(b) In the US Presidential Election in 1948, a major telephone opinion poll predicted a victory of the Republican, Dewey, over the Democrat, Truman.

(c) A headteacher is asked to prepare a report for the school governors on the reasons for absences from school: illness, interviews, truancy and so on. Part of the report is based upon a full investigation of all absences during a week in November.

Sample size

Ensuring that the sample members are selected at random is not the only requirement of a good sample. Sample size is also important – not much information can be obtained from a sample of one, for example! It should be clear that the more information you obtain, the better able you are to make inferences about the population.

4 Using random numbers, select ten samples of size 5 from the sample of students' heights on page 12. Calculate the mean of each sample and the mean and variance of the ten sample means. (Help on how you might select a random sample is provided in the solutions to question 2D.)

5 Repeat question 4 for samples of size 10.

6 Compare and comment on the mean and the variance of the sample means for samples of size 5 and 10.

7 (a) Which size of sample produced better estimates of the population mean (167.4 cm)?

(b) Which distribution of sample means was least variable? Comment on how the difference in spread of the two sets of sample means affects your ability to infer results from a particular sample mean.

The following histograms show possible distributions of samples of size 5 and 10 taken from the students' heights on page 12.

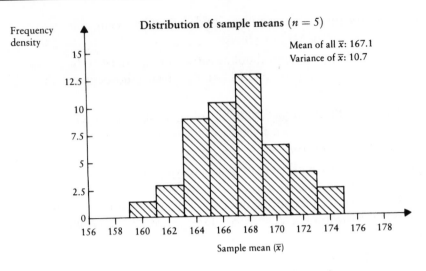

Distribution of sample means $(n = 5)$

Mean of all $\bar{x}$: 167.1
Variance of $\bar{x}$: 10.7

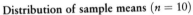

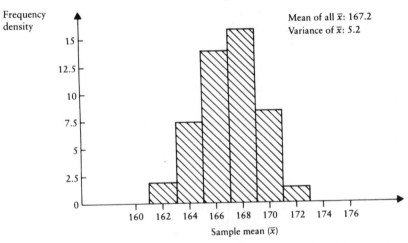

Distribution of sample means $(n = 10)$

Mean of all $\bar{x}$: 167.2
Variance of $\bar{x}$: 5.2

Although each distribution has a mean which is very close to that of the whole population (167.4 cm), the distribution for samples of size 10 has a very much smaller variance than that of the distribution of samples of 5. This implies that a sample mean from a sample of size 10 is *more likely* to be close to the true population mean than one from a sample of size 5. It is clear that this effect will be even more pronounced for a sample of size 20.

A more interesting problem is how large the sample needs to be to give reliable information about the population. Public opinion polls, for example, should always state the sample size as well as the method used to select the sample. The sample size is often about 1000 people.

When studying reports of sampling procedures you must consider both whether the sample has been chosen in a random way and whether it is sufficiently large for any results to be significant.

Canvassing 'everyone' is so costly and time-consuming that sampling is a widespread technique, despite the inevitable problems.

> The sample should be selected at random. Any hint of possible bias should be avoided.
>
> The sample must be large enough to provide sufficiently accurate information about the population.

The concepts relating to sampling techniques and the inference of results from samples will be developed and made more precise in later chapters.

Using the binomial model to test claims based on sample evidence

Using the ideas of this chapter, you can investigate some of the claims typically made in advertising. Suppose, for example, a television commercial states that 8 out of 10 dogs prefer Wolfit dog food. The claim is based upon a particular test in which 8 out of 10 dogs chose Wolfit when given a choice between Wolfit and another dog food.

The manufacturer hopes that you will infer that 80% of all dogs prefer Wolfit!

The evidence here is based on a single sample of 10 dogs: it may not even be a representative sample of all dogs. Even if only 50% of dogs prefer Wolfit, 8 out of 10 dogs choosing Wolfit might not be an unusual occurrence. The possibility that dogs have no preference for either dog food can be modelled by assuming they will choose either one or the other at random. The probability of choosing Wolfit is 0.5 on the basis of this assumption. The probability of 8 or more dogs out of 10 choosing Wolfit can then be obtained from the binomial distribution.

The probability that exactly 8 choose Wolfit is

$$\binom{10}{8}\left(\frac{1}{2}\right)^8\left(\frac{1}{2}\right)^2 = \frac{45}{1024}.$$

If R is the number choosing Wolfit, then the full probability distribution is

r	0	1	2	3	4	5	6	7	8	9	10
$P(R=r)$	$\frac{1}{1024}$	$\frac{10}{1024}$	$\frac{45}{1024}$	$\frac{120}{1024}$	$\frac{210}{1024}$	$\frac{252}{1024}$	$\frac{210}{1024}$	$\frac{120}{1024}$	$\frac{45}{1024}$	$\frac{10}{1024}$	$\frac{1}{1024}$

The result '8 or more out of 10' is only likely to occur in about 5% of all samples of 10 dogs. This is not very likely and suggests that the assumption that the dogs have no preference is wrong. It appears likely that more than 50% of dogs would indeed choose Wolfit.

8 The article below is reprinted from the *Southampton Guardian*.

You throw out monorail idea

By Mark Hodson

COUNCIL plans for a £20m futuristic monorail through the centre of Southampton have been given a thumbs down from city residents

According to a Guardian readers' survey, 90 per cent of people do not want the new 'Metro 2000' system, and almost half would prefer to see the return of trams to the city.

Of those responding, 10 per cent said they want the monorail, 48 per cent want the trams back and 42 per cent said neither idea was worth taking up.

The Metro 2000 would join 13 central stations with electrically-driven remote controlled modules carrying up to 20 people at a time.

The proposals are not yet council policy, but are being used as the basis for discussions with local groups.

A report summarising views of local people will be compiled later this year, and the council is now keen to gauge public response before then.

Tory leader Cllr Norman Best, who has branded the monorail "a gimmick", said the council should think again in the light of the results of our poll.

"These figures do not surprise me at all," he said. "When all these people have taken the trouble to write in, they should be listened to. I am convinced the majority of people in Southampton do not want this monorail, but would prefer to see the return of the trams."

Council leader Alan Whitehead wrote in his introduction to the plans that such an innovation may fundamentally change the face of the city. An understanding and agreement across the city of exactly where we are going and what steps we need to take to get there will immensely strengthen the hand of whoever is charged with taking such decisions."

He says the scheme has met with an enthusiastic response from developers who he hopes will put up the £20m needed.

There will be a public meeting on June 1 when council officers will answer questions about the details of the plans.

WHAT YOU SAY:

● "A definite NO to the city wrecking, crazy idea of a monorail, which would benefit no-one," said J Gubb, Bedford Place.

● "I am against the monorail, trams and any other gimmicks by aspiring Westminster residents. Surely the priority must be to improve existing services," said S Hunter, Radstock Road.

● "Trams would add to noise pollution. A monorail would be much more exciting and would attract visitors to the city," said M Buckle of Rushington Lane.

● "A monorail is a ridiculous idea. It would completely ruin the appearance of the city. The supporting structures would certainly look awful, and the noise for those people working in adjoining buildings would be unbearable," said Mrs J Draper of Chilworth.

● "Bring back the trams. They are cheap to ride, cheap to run and efficient as transport can be," said Alfred Hole of Peach Road.

● Our poll attracted 48 replies.

(a) Which people would you expect to be in favour of a monorail in the centre of a city?

(b) How many replied and, of those who replied, how many wanted these options?

(i) The monorail   (ii) The trams   (iii) Neither

(c) How do you think the monorail 'poll' was carried out? Would this method introduce bias in the sample? Suggest a better method. What do you understand the word 'bias' to mean?

The article uses the views from a sample of Southampton residents to judge the general support, or lack of support, for the monorail idea. Such sampling is widely used for purposes as varied as market research on proposed new products, establishing views about changes in public services, quality control in manufacturing processes and judging public opinion before elections.

In any sampling procedure it is important that the way the poll is carried out should not introduce bias. For example, a poll conducted by telephone would automatically exclude approximately one fifth of the population. This could be a crucial omission.

The second important consideration for any sampling procedure is connected with the sample size. How reasonable is it to infer from a sample size of only 48 that the majority of the inhabitants of Southampton are opposed to the monorail? Is it possible that the citizens are divided roughly equally on this issue and that the sample result occurred simply by chance?

Again, the probability that such a result could have occurred simply by chance can be calculated using the binomial distribution. If you assume that 50% of the population are in favour of the monorail, the probability that a random sample of 48 shows only 5 or fewer in favour would be

$$\binom{48}{5}\left(\frac{1}{2}\right)^5\left(\frac{1}{2}\right)^{43} + \binom{48}{4}\left(\frac{1}{2}\right)^4\left(\frac{1}{2}\right)^{44} + \ldots + \binom{48}{0}\left(\frac{1}{2}\right)^0\left(\frac{1}{2}\right)^{48}.$$

This would not be easy to calculate!

A computer can be used to **simulate** a poll several times and you can then see from the **simulation** how likely particular occurrences appear to be.

A computer simulation can help you to test conjectures based upon results from a particular sample. You should use the following procedure.

- First make an assumption about the parent population to enable you to simulate the taking of samples. You might, for example, assume that 50% of the population support a particular measure such as the construction of a monorail.

- Next, simulate the selection of a large number of samples of the same size as the actual sample. This can be done on a spreadsheet-based simulation, for example the 'Letters simulation' worksheet in the BINO.XLS file of the DISCUS package. (See page iv for information about DISCUS.)

- From the distribution of the simulated samples, use the actual sample to judge the reasonableness of the original assumption.

The result of a simulation, where 100 samples of size 48 were taken, is shown below.

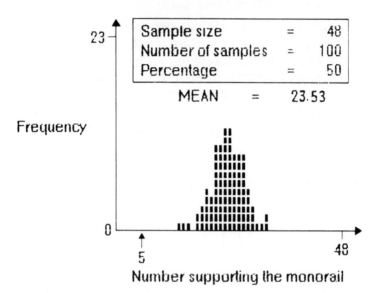

Distribution of simulated samples

Sample size	=	48
Number of samples	=	100
Percentage	=	50

MEAN   =   23.53

Frequency

Number supporting the monorail

9   Do you think the initial assumption of 50% supporting the monorail is likely, considering the simulation result?

10 Comment on the results of the poll in the newspaper article in the light of the evidence provided by the simulation.

11 Suppose that the 48 randomly selected *Southampton Guardian* respondents had contained 22 people in favour of the monorail. What conclusion would you reach in this case?

Remember that you must *always* consider how the original data in any sample are collected. If the method of collection is suspect and likely to lead to distorted results, then no amount of analysis of the data will correct matters. Poor data collection will undermine any survey.

Exercise C (answers p. 107)

1   A person claims that he can predict which way a coin will land, either heads or tails. In eight throws he gets it right on six occasions.

Calculate, on the basis of a binomial model, the probability of these events occurring.

(a) Getting six correct out of eight

(b) Getting six or more correct out of eight

Do you think the result supports his claim? Explain your answer.

2 A blind tasting is organised to see if people can tell the difference between two different brands of orange juice. They have ten 'tastes'. On each occasion they have to say whether it is juice A or juice B. On how many occasions would you expect them to get it right before you were reasonably convinced that they could actually tell the difference?

3 (a) If a coin comes down heads three times out of ten throws, would you suspect it was biased? Explain your answer.

(b) A coin is tossed 100 times and comes down heads 30 times. Would you suspect this coin to be biased?

Comment on your conclusions to (a) and (b).

After working through this chapter you should

1 appreciate the need for **sampling** and for ensuring that the sampling procedure does not introduce **bias**

2 know how to check **significance** either by simulation or, when appropriate, by using the binomial distribution

3 be aware that, as the sample size increases, the distribution of the sample mean becomes increasingly clustered around the true value of the population mean

4 know *when* and *how* to apply binomial models to appropriate situations

5 understand the notation $\binom{n}{r}$ and be able to work out values

6 know that, if the random variable R is the number of occurrences, r, of an event in n independent trials, then

$$P(R = r) = \binom{n}{r} p^r q^{n-r}$$

where p is the probability of the event and $q = 1 - p$.

2 Continuous random variables

A The uniform or rectangular distribution (answers p. 108)

1 x is the discrete random variable 'The score on a fair six-sided die'. Give the probability distribution for x.

All you needed to do here was give a probability for each of six separate values.

Imagine now that instead of a six-sided die you had a perfect cylinder to be rolled gently along a hard surface and that the circumference was marked evenly from 0 to 6 (at the same point as zero).

Suppose that S is the (continuous) random variable 'Score on rolling the cylinder' and that the score is determined by the point in contact with the surface when the cylinder comes to a stop (all points having equal probability).

As there are now an infinite number of possible points each individual point must have a probability of zero. Clearly, however, the cylinder must stop somewhere!

We can represent the probability distribution of S by a graph.

S represents the random variable which can take values in the range $0 \leqslant s < 6$.

The *area* under the graph is used to represent the probability of S taking any particular range of values.

Notice that it is conventional to use capital letters for random variables and lower case letters for their values.

2D S **must** take a value in the range $0 \leqslant s < 6$.
(a) What must the area under the graph between 0 and 6 be?
(b) What is the value of h on the graph?

f (s) is called the **probability density function** (p.d.f.) of the random variable S.

In this case we can define f(s) by

$$f(s) = \begin{cases} \frac{1}{6} & 0 \leqslant s < 6 \\ 0 & \text{all other values of } s \end{cases}$$

Exercise A (answers p. 108)

1   For the random variable S (as defined above) find the following
    probabilities.
    (a) $P(0 \leqslant S < 3)$ (b) $P(S < 0)$ (c) $P(S \geqslant 4)$ (d) $P(S \geqslant 6)$
    (e) $P(1 \leqslant S < 2)$ (f) $P(-1 \leqslant S < 2\frac{1}{2})$ (g) $P(S < 2\frac{1}{2})$

2   X is a random variable defined such that X can take any value in the
    range $-2 \leqslant x < 2$ with equal probability.
    (a) Define the probability density function $f(x)$ for X.
    (b) Find $P(X \geqslant 1)$.
    (c) Find $P(-2 \leqslant X < 0.5)$.

3E If question 2(b) was changed to read 'Find $P(X > 1)$' would it make
    any difference to the probability?
    Explain your answer.

B   **Some notation** (answers p. 108)

In Exercise A both S and X are said to have **continuous
uniform distributions** (sometimes also called Rectangular
distributions) and we can write $S \sim U(0, 6)$ and $X \sim U(-2, 2)$
respectively where '$\sim$' means 'has the distribution'.

> In general if a continuous random variable X is such that
> $X \sim U(a, b)$,
>
> $$\text{then } f(x) = \begin{cases} \dfrac{1}{b-a} & \text{for } a \leqslant x < b \\[2mm] 0 & \text{for all other values of } x. \end{cases}$$

Exercise B (answers p. 108)

1   $T \sim U(5, 10)$
    Find these probabilities.
    (a) $P(5 \leqslant T \leqslant 10)$ (b) $P(T < 7)$ (c) $P(6 \leqslant T < 8)$
    (d) $P(T > 7)$ (e) $P(T > 9.5)$ (f) $P(T > 10)$

2   $W \sim U(-3, 3)$
    Find these probabilities.
    (a) $P(W < 0)$ (b) $P(-1 \leqslant W < 1)$ (c) $P(2 \leqslant W)$
    (d) $P(W \leqslant 2)$ (e) $P(W < -2.5)$ (f) $P(W < -3.5)$

C **Other probability density functions** (answers p. 108)

Not all continuous random variables have probability distributed uniformly.

Consider for example the following graph.

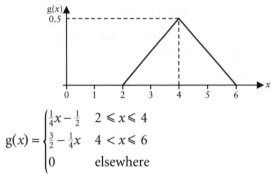

$$g(x) = \begin{cases} \frac{1}{4}x - \frac{1}{2} & 2 \leqslant x \leqslant 4 \\ \frac{3}{2} - \frac{1}{4}x & 4 < x \leqslant 6 \\ 0 & \text{elsewhere} \end{cases}$$

1 (a) Find the total area under the graph.

   (b) Given that area represents probability, why is this the only possible area for the graph of a probability distribution?

The **probability** of a continuous random variable x taking values in any particular range can be shown by the area under a positive graph $f(x)$ within the given range.

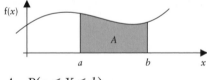

$$A = P(a \leqslant X \leqslant b)$$

● Using calculus we can write

$$P(a \leqslant X \leqslant b) = \int_{a}^{b} f(x)dx$$

● $f(x)$ is called the **probability density function** (p.d.f.).
● For a valid p.d.f. the **total area** under $f(x)$ must be **1** (representing the certainty of some value occurring).

● Using calculus $\displaystyle\int_{-\infty}^{\infty} f(x)dx = 1$.

Exercise C (answers p. 108)

1 For the continuous random variable X, represented by the probability density function $g(x)$ on the previous page find these probabilities.

(a) $P(X \leqslant 4)$ (b) $P(X \leqslant 3)$ (c) $P(3 < X \leqslant 5)$ (d) $P(X < 2)$

2 (a) Confirm that $f(y) = \begin{cases} \frac{1}{2}y & 0 \leqslant y \leqslant 2 \\ 0 & \text{elsewhere} \end{cases}$

is a valid (possible) probability density function (p.d.f.) for a random variable Y.

(b) Find $P(Y \leqslant 1)$.

(c) Find $P(Y \geqslant \frac{1}{2})$.

(d) Find $P(\frac{1}{2} \leqslant Y < 1\frac{1}{2})$.

3 A random variable X has the following p.d.f.

$$f(x) = \begin{cases} \frac{1}{4} & 1 \leqslant x \leqslant 2 \\ \frac{1}{2} & 2 < x \leqslant 3 \\ 2 - \frac{1}{2}x & 3 < x \leqslant 4 \\ 0 & \text{elsewhere} \end{cases}$$

(a) Sketch a graph of $f(x)$ and demonstrate, by finding the area under the graph, that $f(x)$ is a valid p.d.f.

(b) Find $P(X \leqslant 1)$.

(c) Find $P(1 \leqslant X < 3\frac{1}{2})$.

(d) Find $P(X \geqslant 2\frac{1}{2})$.

4 This is the graph for a p.d.f. $g(x)$.

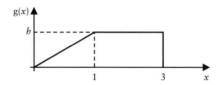

(a) Find h.

(b) Write down a full definition for $g(x)$.

(c) Find   (i) $P(0.5 \leqslant X \leqslant 2.5)$

           (ii) $P(X < 2)$

After working through this chapter you should

1   understand how a probability density function (p.d.f.) represents a continuous random variable

2   be able to draw a p.d.f. from a full definition of it

3   be able to give a full definition of a p.d.f. from its graph

4   know that the area under the graph of a p.d.f. equals 1

5   be able to find probabilities that a variable will lie between specified values, given a p.d.f.

3 The Normal distribution

A Variability (answers p. 109)

Variability is an important feature of life – without it there would be little call for a study of probability and statistics! In this chapter you will consider whether there are patterns in this variability and whether or not you can describe the patterns mathematically.

Stand on any busy street corner and you cannot fail to notice the immense variety in the human form.

1D Suppose you were asked to sample the heights of 100 adult males and draw a histogram. Jot down the rough shape of the histogram you would expect.

Why would you expect to get the shape you have drawn?

2 These are the weights of 100 2p coins, in grams.

7.15	7.08	7.09	7.05	7.33
7.05	7.09	7.12	7.18	7.19
7.08	7.09	7.09	7.20	7.07
7.12	7.11	7.26	6.86	7.14
6.80	7.11	6.99	7.05	7.11
7.27	6.97	7.40	7.12	7.44
7.17	7.17	7.05	7.18	7.13
7.11	7.19	7.16	7.04	7.15
7.11	7.01	7.21	7.02	7.05
7.03	7.22	7.30	7.18	7.14
7.08	7.06	7.30	7.12	7.04
7.11	7.16	7.07	7.22	7.18
7.24	7.20	7.09	7.13	7.11
6.95	7.01	7.18	7.23	7.16
7.00	7.08	7.03	7.04	7.18
7.17	7.12	7.14	7.13	7.18
7.19	7.07	6.98	7.22	7.15
7.34	7.18	7.21	7.06	7.24
6.98	7.25	7.19	7.29	7.17
7.20	7.04	7.17	7.19	7.11

(a) Draw a frequency distribution diagram for the data and comment on its shape.

(b) Use the frequency distribution and the statistics functions on your calculator to show that the mean and standard deviation of the weights in grams of the 2p coins are 7.13 and 0.10 (correct to 2 d.p.).

(c) What proportion of the observations (**approximately**) are in these intervals?

    (i)   Within ±1 standard deviation of the mean

    (ii) More than 2 standard deviations from the mean.

Many frequency distributions look like those for the weights of coins.

● The frequency distribution is approximately symmetrical.

● Most of the values are grouped around the mean.

● Values a long way from the mean are not very likely.

It is interesting to consider whether the distributions of other variable quantities have the same or similar shapes.

3 Choose **one** of the data sets A to E on pages 27 to 29 making sure that each of the data sets is considered by someone in the class.

(a) Draw a frequency distribution to represent the data. You should collect the data into groups whose widths are all 1 standard deviation. For example, if the data have mean 10.3 and standard deviation 0.2, use intervals of:

$$... 9.9 - 10.1 \quad 10.1 - 10.3 \quad 10.3 - 10.5 ...$$

(b) What proportion of the observations for your chosen data set are in these intervals?

    (i)   Within 1 standard deviation of the mean

    (ii) Between 1 and 2 standard deviations above the mean

    (iii) More than 3 standard deviations away from the mean

(c) Obtain, from others in your class, results for all the data sets and copy and complete the table below.

Data set	Approximate proportion of observations within n standard deviations of the mean			
	±1	±2	±3	Beyond 3
A				
B				
C				
D				
E				

Data set A

Times (in seconds) taken for 10 oscillations of a 50 cm long pendulum, initial angle 10°

$n = 100$, mean = 14.52, standard deviation = 0.072

14.48	14.51	14.60	14.36	14.42	14.53	14.52	14.55
14.60	14.68	14.46	14.53	14.52	14.44	14.51	14.54
14.50	14.70	14.51	14.53	14.38	14.61	14.50	14.52
14.41	14.48	14.48	14.55	14.62	14.63	14.57	14.58
14.43	14.60	14.58	14.59	14.42	14.51	14.57	14.44
14.56	14.58	14.52	14.50	14.45	14.47	14.58	14.48
14.47	14.54	14.60	14.44	14.49	14.53	14.70	14.52
14.53	14.46	14.43	14.52	14.50	14.58	14.52	14.51
14.45	14.54	14.46	14.62	14.40	14.51	14.52	14.54
14.46	14.48	14.59	14.56	14.49	14.57	14.62	14.55
14.65	14.54	14.42	14.50	14.52	14.43	14.33	14.38
14.44	14.48	14.55	14.49	14.49	14.55	14.58	14.55
14.43	14.68	14.48	14.63				

Data set B

Times (in seconds) taken for 10 oscillations of a 50 cm long pendulum, initial angle 45°

$n = 100$, mean = 15.07, standard deviation = 0.066

15.11	15.17	15.12	15.01	15.17	15.08	15.02	15.07
15.04	14.99	15.07	15.00	15.11	14.97	15.07	15.06
15.13	15.00	15.06	15.18	15.05	15.05	15.11	15.10
15.12	15.15	15.08	15.15	15.14	15.09	15.09	15.13
15.09	14.98	15.13	15.02	15.01	15.11	15.12	15.09
15.13	15.10	14.90	14.95	15.03	15.05	15.03	15.10
15.07	15.12	14.97	15.13	15.09	15.17	15.07	15.02
15.11	14.98	15.06	15.05	15.05	15.07	15.07	15.03
15.02	14.98	15.05	14.98	15.12	15.01	15.12	15.09
15.11	15.06	15.05	15.14	15.01	15.17	15.03	15.18
15.12	14.99	15.20	15.05	14.91	15.04	15.06	14.99
15.15	15.02	15.28	15.01	15.13	15.11	15.09	15.20
15.10	15.01	15.02	14.99				

Data set C
Heights (in centimetres) of male sixth-formers
$n = 150$,   mean = 173.5,   standard deviation = 6.47

170.1	165.2	175.1	172.2	172.7	169.6	172.9	176.7
178.1	178.2	173.0	182.0	160.8	168.7	177.2	169.4
176.6	163.7	162.8	169.6	173.3	181.0	179.5	163.4
178.8	182.6	163.6	179.3	180.2	181.4	164.9	183.8
173.3	167.9	174.1	180.4	175.2	175.0	183.6	168.7
175.3	171.0	160.2	170.5	175.1	163.7	168.2	182.3
165.9	174.8	170.0	163.6	168.8	164.9	168.9	184.9
171.4	170.6	171.0	177.9	171.2	180.1	179.6	168.8
184.3	175.6	167.4	176.6	176.1	173.7	168.5	173.9
175.9	178.8	177.6	167.1	180.9	166.2	176.3	171.1
175.0	172.3	162.2	181.5	173.2	177.2	172.5	170.3
169.0	172.2	173.1	188.0	178.9	175.8	174.1	175.5
167.1	181.1	171.8	173.0	160.5	186.3	163.7	170.5
159.9	175.0	189.1	178.4	182.9	170.0	176.6	163.3
168.5	172.4	173.7	167.9	176.4	175.1	171.7	179.7
167.8	179.4	179.4	172.0	178.3	178.0	178.1	172.0
179.7	186.1	174.8	173.7	181.2	171.0	163.7	163.6
179.0	162.7	178.4	176.3	167.0	183.3	181.9	159.9
171.3	170.0	185.9	179.9	165.2	170.6		

Data set D
Heights (in centimetres) of female sixth-formers
$n = 150$,   mean = 161.4,   standard deviation = 6.59

168.1	161.1	150.5	166.7	171.9	163.0	159.1	170.1
160.3	171.8	160.3	179.3	162.8	155.3	156.8	163.2
158.6	156.2	175.6	153.9	171.8	154.9	166.7	160.0
155.4	164.7	152.0	157.0	159.2	165.3	163.7	153.2
157.3	172.9	164.6	151.5	166.9	179.6	161.5	164.7
164.4	167.3	156.9	155.5	164.4	165.6	165.5	157.4
168.8	150.4	171.2	160.4	175.7	152.0	165.3	162.5
158.7	163.6	166.3	160.7	162.9	156.2	159.3	156.7
167.1	153.7	172.3	160.2	164.5	156.8	159.4	157.2
159.5	150.3	166.0	173.8	168.3	168.3	161.2	156.3
162.9	161.7	155.0	159.8	152.9	168.9	156.3	176.4
155.7	154.8	159.4	152.9	160.0	159.1	157.6	160.8
150.2	157.7	166.0	160.9	158.0	163.8	159.9	170.4
157.0	153.0	166.5	165.4	158.5	164.8	155.7	169.4
164.2	157.4	162.3	141.1	164.8	162.2	154.2	156.8
169.3	164.1	156.6	158.3	157.0	162.7	167.3	158.9
162.3	153.8	146.4	166.2	170.5	154.7	162.1	164.6
155.9	154.6	157.3	164.1	165.7	160.0	168.8	161.1
157.0	168.3	155.1	162.5	160.1	153.7		

Data set E

Times (in seconds) between the arrivals of cars at a road junction

$n = 243$, mean = 44.1, standard deviation = 44.0

55	129	6	66	3	107	7	38
36	18	110	35	58	87	12	110
32	7	104	20	36	147	95	35
11	67	0	51	42	14	201	74
16	28	2	52	21	25	153	7
23	14	11	162	18	2	2	20
135	29	24	16	1	4	3	100
35	3	39	6	3	20	103	87
5	40	79	76	4	54	30	31
8	2	24	7	1	5	105	3
54	105	70	53	12	54	100	152
6	214	57	19	98	76	7	97
7	26	84	24	33	4	42	100
43	8	7	5	13	67	37	6
33	15	27	25	30	71	5	12
6	19	11	129	89	5	34	75
18	153	97	16	14	110	31	112
11	56	84	155	175	33	19	19
23	13	12	62	9	4	11	0
7	88	18	82	31	2	45	16
29	21	81	15	249	25	107	21
59	26	58	33	18	25	57	3
45	40	11	12	5	22	6	16
84	35	3	80	70	41	31	38
119	8	115	41	41	32	67	2
19	10	75	71	3	11	12	2
29	51	42	10	89	32	14	45
68	34	36	139	4	25	4	62
20	25	4	128	42	4	15	136
17	21	43	2	84	45	33	78
4	27	54					

4D | Comment on the shapes of the various distributions considered in question 3, describing their similarities and differences.

Which distributions have the same shape as that for the weights of coins?

Although the data sets are of different sorts of observation the distributions have approximately the same shape (data set E is the exception). Most of the values are near the mean, which is in the middle, and the distribution is roughly symmetrical. It is often described as being 'bell-shaped'.

Many (but not all) distributions which occur in statistics turn out to be approximately bell-shaped.

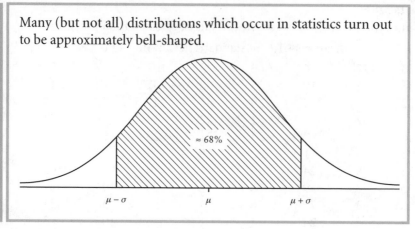

As well as the distributions having similar shapes the proportion of the data contained within 1 standard deviation of the mean is approximately the same (about 68%) for each data set.

Your work so far might lead you to suspect that there is, or might be, a common underlying distribution for various physical situations. If there is, then perhaps it is possible to find a suitable mathematical model to describe it. This approach is pursued first by considering a method of **standardising the data** and then by making the **area** under each histogram independent of the total frequency.

Standardising the data

A group of students sat examinations in both mathematics and economics.

5D | Debbie scored 64 for mathematics and 78 for economics. Which was the better result?

The class results were as follows:

● The mathematics scores had mean 54 and standard deviation 4.8.

● The economics scores had mean 68 and standard deviation 8.0.

In comparing two examination scores, working out how far each is above or below the mean takes account of the difference in means, but not the difference in spread. To take account of this, you can measure the distance from the mean in **units of standard deviation**. So, for Debbie,

● her mathematics score was $\dfrac{(64 - 54)}{4.8} = 2.08$ standard deviations above the mean

● her economics score was $\dfrac{(78 - 68)}{8.0} = 1.25$ standard deviations above the mean.

These results, 2.08 and 1.25, are called the **standardised** scores, and give a simple method of comparison. The higher the standardised score, the better the *relative* examination performance.

Standardised data is often denoted by the variable Z. (It is sometimes referred to as the z-score.) Remember that it is conventional to use capital letters for random variables and lower case letters for their values.

> Suppose a data set has mean $\bar{x}$ and standard deviation s. The standardised value of an observation x is z, where
> $$z = \frac{x - \bar{x}}{s}$$

Suppose eight competitors in a school quiz programme have scores of 9, 9, 10, 12, 14, 16, 16 and 18.

The mean score is $\frac{104}{8} = 13$. The standard deviation is 3.28 (to 3 s.f.).

The **standardised** form of the score of 9 is $\frac{9 - 13}{3.28} = -1.22$ (to 3 s.f.).

This means that the score of 9 is 1.22 standard deviation units *below* the mean.

The full set of standardised scores is given in this table.

Original score	9	9	10	12	14	16	16	18
Standardised score	−1.22	−1.22	−0.915	−0.305	0.305	0.915	0.915	1.52

The mean of the standardised scores for the data set is 0.00, and the standard deviation is 1.00 (to 3 s.f.).

The calculations could be performed conveniently on a spreadsheet or a statistics package on the computer. You might like to try this or you could write a short program to do the job for you on a programmable calculator or computer. Your calculator will probably also have 'built in' statistics functions which you can use.

6 The mean and the standard deviation of the standardised scores are approximately 0 and 1 respectively for this data set.
Investigate other small data sets and comment on your findings.

> A standardised data set has a mean of 0 and a standard deviation of 1.

Exercise A (answers p. 110)

1   Standardise these.

   (a) A score of 6 from a population of mean 8 and standard deviation 2

   (b) A score of 1.45 from a population of mean 2.3 and standard deviation 0.3

   (c) A score of 3.4 from a population of mean 0 and standard deviation 3.4

   (d) A score of x from a population of mean m and standard deviation d

2   The results for a large group of students in mathematics had a mean of 54 and a standard deviation of 4.8. For economics, there was a mean of 68 and a standard deviation of 8.

   (a) Compare the results of the following students in mathematics and economics by calculating their standardised scores.

	Mathematics	Economics
Karen	58	71
Soujit	41	41
Melanie	54	68
Chris	20	25

   (b) Nafisha did equally well in economics and mathematics. If she scored 64 marks in mathematics, what was her economics mark?

   (c) Mark obtained the same mark in each subject, and his performances were equally good. What marks did he get?

3   A population of men has a mean height of 5 ft 8 in and standard deviation 2.8 inches. A population of women has a mean height of 5 ft 6 in and standard deviation 2.4 inches.

   (a) Which is taller (relative to his or her own population), a 5 ft 7 in man or a 5 ft 5 in woman?

   (b) What woman's height, to the nearest inch, is equivalent to that of a 6 ft man?

4E Prove that, for any standardised data set, the mean is zero and the standard deviation is one.

B Considering the area (answers p. 111)

All standardised data sets have mean 0 and variance 1. To make comparisons between data sets even more meaningful you can also make the area under the graph of each distribution the same.

You should recall that, for a histogram,

$$\text{height of a block} = \text{frequency density} = \frac{\text{frequency}}{\text{width of interval}}.$$

For example, consider the data below for the weights of 100 2p coins.

Weight (g)	6.8–7.0	7.0–7.1	7.1–7.2	7.2–7.3	7.3–7.5
Frequency	8	29	46	12	5

This is the histogram.

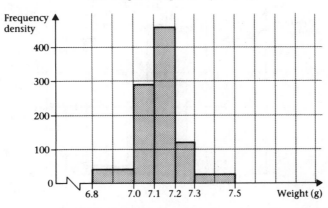

The weights of 2p coins ($n = 100$)

1D
(a) What does the **area** of each block represent?

(b) What does the total area of all the blocks represent?

The area of a frequency density histogram is dependent on the total frequency. Since this is different in each case, each histogram will have a different area.

To make the area independent of total frequency, consider the **relative frequency** in each class, which is simply the frequency for each class divided by the total frequency.

$$\text{Relative frequency} = \frac{\text{frequency for the class}}{\text{total frequency}}.$$

The height of each block on the histogram now becomes

$$\text{height} = \frac{\text{relative frequency}}{\text{width of interval}} = \textbf{relative frequency density}$$

The **relative frequency density histogram** for the coins can now be drawn using the data given below.

Weight (g)	6.8–7.0	7.0–7.1	7.1–7.2	7.2–7.3	7.3–7.5
Frequency	8	29	46	12	5
Relative frequency	0.08	0.29	0.46	0.12	0.05
Relative frequency density	0.4	2.9	4.6	1.2	0.25

Height of block

$$\text{Relative frequency} = \frac{\text{frequency}}{\text{total frequency}} = \frac{8}{100}$$

$$\frac{\text{Relative frequency}}{\text{density}} = \frac{\text{relative frequency}}{\text{width of block}} = \frac{0.46}{0.1} = 4.6$$

The weights of 2p coins ($n = 100$)

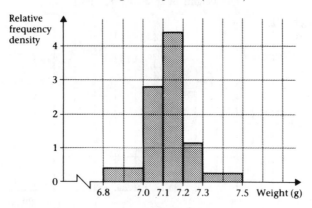

2D
(a) What is the total relative frequency?
(b) What is the total area of the histogram?
(c) Draw the relative frequency density histogram for one of the data sets A–E from pages 27–29. Confirm that the total area is 1.

A relative frequency density histogram has a total area of 1.

The 'Normal' curve

You have seen that many, *but not all*, data sets have an approximately bell-shaped histogram. This has been observed and noted by many mathematicians, among them Carl Friedrich Gauss (1777–1855) and Abraham de Moivre (1667–1754).

Gauss noted that 'errors' in scientific measurement produced the bell-shaped histogram. He hypothesised that measurements which are subject to accidental or random effects will always produce a histogram of this shape.

The histogram below illustrates a very large data set where the data are grouped into small block widths. The data represents the mass (kg) of new-born babies.

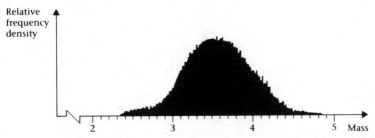

This histogram has a fairly smooth bell shape and it is natural to draw a smooth curve through the tops of the blocks, ironing out the bumps.

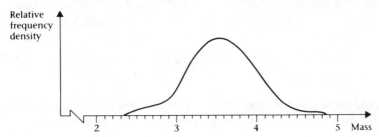

You can model this curve approximately with the graph of a symmetrical function.

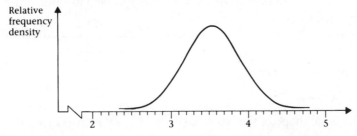

The sketch above shows the bell-shaped distribution which has provided the skeleton shape for many distributions. A mathematical model for such distributions was developed by de Moivre and by Pierre-Simon Laplace (1749–1827). It was upon this model that Gauss, de Moivre and Laplace based their theory of errors. For this reason, the bell-shaped curve is sometimes called the 'Gaussian error curve'. It is more commonly known as the **Normal curve**.

When a data set has been standardised, the particular Normal curve which models the data takes on a number of important properties. The normal curve for standardised data is called the **Standard Normal curve**.

3D | Describe the shape and area properties of the Standard Normal curve.

The Standard Normal distribution has mean 0 and standard deviation 1.

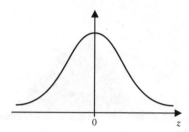

The area under the curve is 1.

To make full use of this mathematical model to describe data sets you need to identify the function involved. This is investigated next.

4D   (a) Plot the graphs of functions of the form

$$f(x) = ke^{-\frac{1}{2}x^2}$$

and show that functions of this form have the same basic **shape** as the Normal curve. Consider different values of k, including negative values.

(b) What important **area** property should a function for the Normal distribution possess? How does this help in finding the required value of k?

The function f, where

$$f(x) = ke^{-\frac{1}{2}x^2}$$

has the basic shape of the Normal curve. (k is a positive constant, as yet undetermined.)

Sketches of the graph of f for various values of k are shown below.

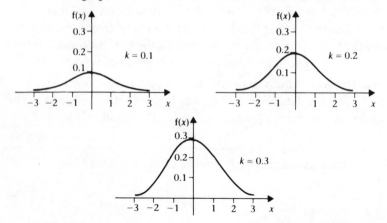

Each curve has the correct shape. It is necessary only to find which curve encloses an area of 1.

5 Consider the graph of $g(x) = e^{-\frac{1}{2}x^2}$.

   (a) Use a suitable graphing program, or write a short program for your calculator, to estimate the total area under the curve.

   (b) Estimate the proportion of the area under the curve between these values.

      (i) 0 and 1   (ii) 1 and 2   (iii) 2 and 3

   (c) Write down the corresponding proportions between these values.

      (i) 0 and −1   (ii) −1 and −2   (iii) −2 and −3

6 Compare your results for data sets A–D (from Section A of this chapter) with your answers to question 5.

7 The total area under $e^{-\frac{1}{2}x^2}$ was estimated in question 5(a). Try other functions $ke^{-\frac{1}{2}x^2}$ for various k until you find the value of k which makes the total area equal to 1.

In order to model the relative frequency density histograms for the data sets, the total area under the curve must equal 1.

The numerical methods you have just employed give a value for k of approximately 0.4. In fact, it can be shown that the precise value for k is $\dfrac{1}{\sqrt{2\pi}}$.

> The equation of the Standard Normal curve is
>
> $$f(x) = \frac{1}{\sqrt{2\pi}} e^{-\frac{1}{2}x^2}.$$

Using the Normal distribution

You have seen how the Normal curve can be used as a model for the distribution of a number of continuous variables. The following example shows how you can use this information.

Example 1

Over a long period of time a farmer notes that the eggs produced by his chickens have a mean weight of 60 g, and a standard deviation of 15 g. If eggs are classified by weight and small eggs are those having a weight of less than 45 g, then what proportion of his eggs will be classified as small?

Solution

(a) *Assume* that the distribution of the weight of the eggs is Normal, having mean 60 g and standard deviation 15 g.

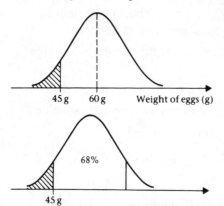

45 g is 1 standard deviation below this mean. You know that roughly 68% of the weights will be within ±1 standard deviation of the mean.

From the diagram you can see that about 16% of his eggs will be small.

8D Use your knowledge of areas under the Normal curve to find the proportion of eggs having weights between 60 g and 75 g.

You saw in *Methods* that relative frequency provides an estimate of probability.

The standardised Normal function, which you have used to model data sets, is also known as the **Normal probability density function**.

With relative frequency density histograms, the area of a block represents the relative frequency of occurrence of the values in the particular interval.

For the Normal distribution, the area shaded is the probability of obtaining a value of x between a and b.

$$\text{Area} = P(a \leqslant x \leqslant b)$$

It is possible to obtain any such area by numerical integration in a similar way to that which you used when investigating the mathematical form of the Normal function.

Exercise B (answers p. 112)

1 Copy and complete the table, which gives the approximate area under

$$f(x) = \frac{1}{\sqrt{2\pi}}\, e^{-\frac{1}{2}x^2}$$ between the limits a and b as shown.

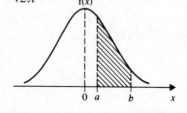

a	b	Area
0	1	
1	2	
2	3	

2 Use the symmetry property of the curve to write down the areas enclosed between ±1, ±2, ±3 standard deviations of the mean.

3 For the Standard Normal curve write down estimates of the probability of obtaining a value of x which is in these intervals.

(a) Between ±1 standard deviation of the mean

(b) More than 2 standard deviations above the mean

(c) More than 3 standard deviations above the mean (Be careful how you calculate this!)

C Tables for the Normal function (answers p. 112)

Using numerical methods, accurate tables such as the one on the next page have been constructed for the area under the Normal curve. Some tables show five places of decimals.

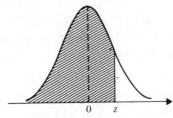

The table gives the area to the left of (or below) any given z-value. z is the number of standard deviation units from the mean value.

For example, from the table you can see that the area to the left of $z = 2$ is 0.977 (to 3 s.f.).

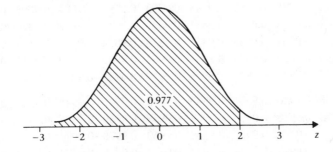

0.977

1D Using the information in the diagram above, what other areas can you find?

z	0.00	0.01	0.02	0.03	0.04	0.05	0.06	0.07	0.08	0.09
0.0	0.5000	0.5040	0.5080	0.5120	0.5160	0.5199	0.5239	0.5279	0.5319	0.5359
0.1	0.5398	0.5438	0.5478	0.5517	0.5557	0.5596	0.5636	0.5675	0.5714	0.5753
0.2	0.5793	0.5832	0.5871	0.5910	0.5948	0.5987	0.6026	0.6064	0.6103	0.6141
0.3	0.6179	0.6217	0.6255	0.6293	0.6331	0.6368	0.6406	0.6443	0.6480	0.6517
0.4	0.6554	0.6591	0.6628	0.6664	0.6700	0.6736	0.6772	0.6808	0.6844	0.6879
0.5	0.6915	0.6950	0.6985	0.7019	0.7054	0.7088	0.7123	0.7157	0.7190	0.7224
0.6	0.7257	0.7291	0.7324	0.7357	0.7389	0.7422	0.7454	0.7486	0.7517	0.7549
0.7	0.7580	0.7611	0.7642	0.7673	0.7704	0.7734	0.7764	0.7794	0.7823	0.7852
0.8	0.7881	0.7910	0.7939	0.7967	0.7995	0.8023	0.8051	0.8078	0.8106	0.8133
0.9	0.8159	0.8186	0.8212	0.8238	0.8264	0.8289	0.8315	0.8340	0.8365	0.8389
1.0	0.8413	0.8438	0.8461	0.8485	0.8508	0.8531	0.8554	0.8577	0.8599	0.8621
1.1	0.8643	0.8665	0.8686	0.8708	0.8729	0.8749	0.8770	0.8790	0.8810	0.8830
1.2	0.8849	0.8869	0.8888	0.8907	0.8925	0.8944	0.8962	0.8980	0.8997	0.9015
1.3	0.9032	0.9049	0.9066	0.9082	0.9099	0.9115	0.9131	0.9147	0.9162	0.9177
1.4	0.9192	0.9207	0.9222	0.9236	0.9251	0.9265	0.9279	0.9292	0.9306	0.9319
1.5	0.9332	0.9345	0.9357	0.9370	0.9382	0.9394	0.9406	0.9418	0.9429	0.9441
1.6	0.9452	0.9463	0.9474	0.9484	0.9495	0.9505	0.9515	0.9525	0.9535	0.9545
1.7	0.9554	0.9564	0.9573	0.9582	0.9591	0.9599	0.9608	0.9616	0.9625	0.9633
1.8	0.9641	0.9649	0.9656	0.9664	0.9671	0.9678	0.9686	0.9693	0.9699	0.9706
1.9	0.9713	0.9719	0.9726	0.9732	0.9738	0.9744	0.9750	0.9756	0.9761	0.9767
2.0	0.9772	0.9778	0.9783	0.9788	0.9793	0.9798	0.9803	0.9808	0.9812	0.9817
2.1	0.9821	0.9826	0.9830	0.9834	0.9838	0.9842	0.9846	0.9850	0.9854	0.9857
2.2	0.9861	0.9864	0.9868	0.9871	0.9875	0.9878	0.9881	0.9884	0.9887	0.9890
2.3	0.9893	0.9896	0.9898	0.9901	0.9904	0.9906	0.9909	0.9911	0.9913	0.9916
2.4	0.9918	0.9920	0.9922	0.9925	0.9927	0.9929	0.9931	0.9932	0.9934	0.9936
2.5	0.9938	0.9940	0.9941	0.9943	0.9945	0.9946	0.9948	0.9949	0.9951	0.9952
2.6	0.9953	0.9955	0.9956	0.9957	0.9959	0.9960	0.9961	0.9962	0.9963	0.9964
2.7	0.9965	0.9966	0.9967	0.9968	0.9969	0.9970	0.9971	0.9972	0.9973	0.9974
2.8	0.9974	0.9975	0.9976	0.9977	0.9977	0.9978	0.9979	0.9979	0.9980	0.9981
2.9	0.9981	0.9982	0.9982	0.9983	0.9984	0.9984	0.9985	0.9985	0.9986	0.9986
3.0	0.9987	0.9987	0.9987	0.9988	0.9988	0.9989	0.9989	0.9989	0.9990	0.9990
3.1	0.9990	0.9991	0.9991	0.9991	0.9992	0.9992	0.9992	0.9992	0.9993	0.9993
3.2	0.9993	0.9993	0.9994	0.9994	0.9994	0.9994	0.9994	0.9995	0.9995	0.9995
3.3	0.9995	0.9995	0.9995	0.9996	0.9996	0.9996	0.9996	0.9996	0.9996	0.9997
3.4	0.9997	0.9997	0.9997	0.9997	0.9997	0.9997	0.9997	0.9997	0.9997	0.9998

It is convenient to have a shorthand notation for the area under the curve up to a given standardised value z.

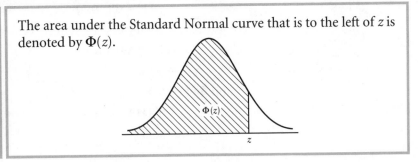

The area under the Standard Normal curve that is to the left of z is denoted by $\Phi(z)$.

When solving problems using the Normal curve you should *always* start with a sketch to help you see exactly what is required.

Example 2

Find these areas under the Standard Normal curve.

(a) Between 1 and 2 standard deviations above the mean
(b) More than 2 standard deviations above the mean
(c) More than 1 standard deviation below the mean
(d) Between −0.5 and +1 standard deviation from the mean

Solution

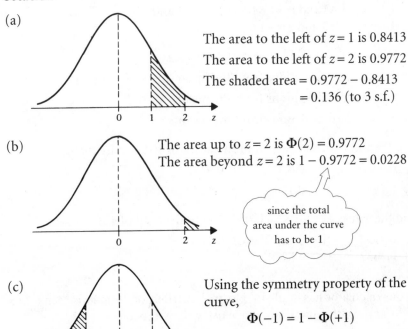

(a)

The area to the left of $z = 1$ is 0.8413
The area to the left of $z = 2$ is 0.9772
The shaded area $= 0.9772 - 0.8413$
$\qquad\qquad\qquad\ = 0.136$ (to 3 s.f.)

(b)

The area up to $z = 2$ is $\Phi(2) = 0.9772$
The area beyond $z = 2$ is $1 - 0.9772 = 0.0228$

since the total area under the curve has to be 1

(c)

Using the symmetry property of the curve,

$$\Phi(-1) = 1 - \Phi(+1)$$
$$= 1 - 0.841$$
$$= 0.159$$

(d)

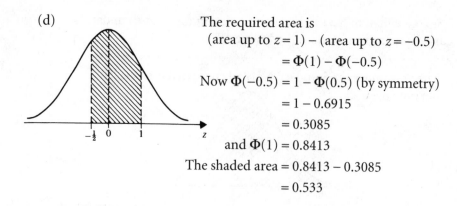

The required area is

(area up to $z = 1$) − (area up to $z = -0.5$)

$$= \Phi(1) - \Phi(-0.5)$$

Now $\Phi(-0.5) = 1 - \Phi(0.5)$ (by symmetry)

$$= 1 - 0.6915$$

$$= 0.3085$$

and $\Phi(1) = 0.8413$

The shaded area $= 0.8413 - 0.3085$

$$= 0.533$$

Exercise C (answers p. 112)

In the questions below, draw sketches showing the relevant area.

1 Using the table of areas under the Standard Normal curve or otherwise, find these areas.

(a) The area between $z = 1$ and $z = 1.5$

(b) The area above these values

(i) $z = 1.5$ (ii) $z = -2$

(c) The area below these values

(i) $z = 1.62$ (ii) $z = 1.47$ (iii) $z = -1.6$

(d) The area enclosed between these values

(i) $z = 1.42$ and $z = 1.84$ (ii) $z = -1$ and $z = 1.5$
(iii) $z = -0.5$ and $z = -1.5$

2 Find the areas enclosed between these values.

(a) ±1 standard deviations from the mean (between $z = 1$ and $z = -1$)

(b) ±2 standard deviations from the mean

(c) ±3 standard deviations from the mean

3 Find the values of z for which the areas to the left of z are these.

(a) 0.8888 (b) 0.670 (c) 0.9332

(d) 0.484 (e) 0.1251

4 Find the values of z for which the areas to the right of z are these.

(a) 0.9357 (b) 0.881 (c) 0.2206
(d) 0.3632 (e) 0.5279

If your calculator has 'built-in' Normal distribution functions then re-do some of the questions above using these functions.

Questions 3 and 4 are easier if you have tables which enable you to look up the standardised z-value *from* the area to its left. Check *your* examination board tables to see if you can do this.

D Solving problems (answers p. 112)

In Section A of this chapter you saw that any Normal curve can be reduced to the Standard Normal curve by standardising the variable. It is therefore possible to use the Standard Normal curve to solve problems for any Normally distributed variable.

For example, figures from the Office for National Statistics show that the mean height of British women (over 16 years) is 160.9 cm and the standard deviation is 6 cm. How would you find the proportion of British women over 166 cm tall?

Always start by illustrating the problem with a sketch.

Note that 166 is about 1 s.d. above the mean.

Assuming that the heights are Normally distributed, approximately 68% of the population are within ±1 s.d. of the mean.

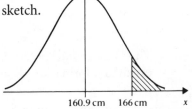

1D Approximately what proportion of women will have a height greater than 166 cm?

You can tackle the problem more precisely in the following way.

First consider the distribution of female heights. The mean height is given as 160.9 cm and the standard deviation is 6 cm. Assume that the distribution of heights is approximately Normal.

To find the proportion of women taller than 166 cm you need to find the area to the right of that value. In order to use the Standard Normal tables, first convert the variable X to a **standardised Normal variable**, Z.

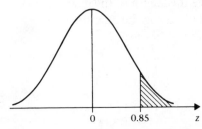

$$z = \frac{166 - 160.9}{6} = \frac{5.1}{6} = 0.85$$

So 166 cm is 0.85 standard deviations above the mean value.

The area to the left of $z = 0.85$ is 0.8023 (from tables).

So about 80.2% of women are shorter than 166 cm. It follows that just less than 20% of women will be taller than 166 cm. This should be reasonably close to your earlier estimate.

If a variable X has a distribution which is modelled by a Normal function, and X has mean μ and standard deviation σ, then

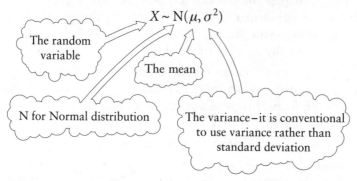

$$X \sim N(\mu, \sigma^2)$$

The random variable

N for Normal distribution

The mean

The variance – it is conventional to use variance rather than standard deviation

This is a standard notation and is a convenient way of providing the essential information about the distribution of the random variable.

> To state that a random variable X has a Normal distribution with mean μ and standard deviation σ, you can write
>
> $$X \sim N(\mu, \sigma^2).$$

Example 3

The length of life (in months) of a certain hair-drier is approximately Normally distributed with mean 90 months and standard deviation 15 months.

(a) Each drier is sold with a 5-year guarantee. What proportion of driers fail before the guarantee expires?

(b) The manufacturer decides to change the length of the guarantee so that no more than 1% of driers fail during the guarantee period. How long should he make the guarantee?

Solution

(a) Let X = length of life of a drier.

Then $X \sim N(90, 15^2)$

5 years is 60 months.

$$z = \frac{60 - 90}{15} = -2.0$$

$$P(X < 60) = \Phi(-2.0)$$
$$= 1 - \Phi(2.0)$$
$$= 1 - 0.9772 = 0.0228$$

So 2.28% of driers will fail during the guarantee period.

(b) Let the length of guarantee be t months.

You require $P(X < t) = 0.01$

First find z where $\Phi(z) = 0.01$

$$\Rightarrow z = -2.33$$

(from tables)

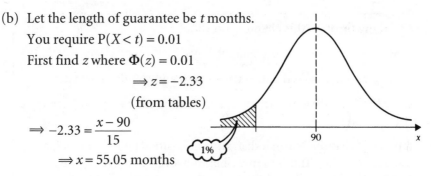

$$\Rightarrow -2.33 = \frac{x - 90}{15}$$

1%

$$\Rightarrow x = 55.05 \text{ months}$$

The manufacturer should give a guarantee of up to 55 months.

Exercise D (answers p. 112)

In each of the following questions, assume that the variable is Normally distributed.

1   The mean IQ of a large number of children aged 12 years is 100 and the standard deviation of the distribution is 15. What percentage of children have an IQ of 132 or more?

2   A machine turns out bolts of mean diameter 1.5 cm and standard deviation 0.01 cm. If bolts measuring over 1.52 cm are rejected as oversize, what proportion are rejected in this way?

3   A machine is used to package sugar in 1 kg bags. The standard deviation is 0.0025 kg. To which mean value should the machine be set so that at least 97% of the bags are over 1 kg in mass?

4   Flour is sold in packets marked 1.5 kg. The average mass is 1.53 kg. What should be the maximum value of the standard deviation to ensure that no more than 1 packet in 200 is underweight?

5   An examiner who regularly assigns 10% As, 20% Bs, 40% Cs, 20% Ds and 10% Es sets an examination in which the average mark is 68. The borderline between Cs and Bs is 78. What is the standard deviation?

6   The mean lifespan for a species of locust is 28 days. If the probability of a locust surviving longer than 31 days is 0.25, estimate the standard deviation of the lifespan.

7   Simply More Pure margarine is sold in tubs with a mean mass of 500 g and standard deviation 4 g. What proportion of tubs will weigh between 498.5 g and 500.5 g?

8   The heights of girls in a particular year group have mean 154.2 cm and standard deviation 5.1 cm. What percentage of the girls are between 150 cm and 155 cm tall?

9   The results of an examination were approximately Normally distributed. 10% of the candidates had more than 70 marks and 20% had fewer than 35 marks. Find the mean and standard deviation.

After working through this chapter you should

1   know how to standardise a data set

2   know that standardised data have mean 0 and standard deviation 1

3   know that a relative frequency density histogram has a total area of 1

4   appreciate that the Normal distribution is often a good model for real data sets. You should remember, however, that even if the distribution *is* bell-shaped the Normal curve may be only an *approximate* fit. The fit should be good enough to obtain useful information from the use of a Normal model.

5   know that the mathematical description for the Standard Normal function, f(x) is

$$f(x) = \frac{1}{\sqrt{2\pi}}\, e^{-\frac{1}{2}x^2}$$

6   know that the area under the Standard Normal curve is 1

7   know that the Standard Normal distribution has mean 0 and standard deviation 1

8   know that, for observations that can be modelled with a Normal distribution, about 68% of all observations lie within ±1 standard deviation of the mean and about 95% are within 2 standard deviations

9   know how to use tables of the area under the **Standard Normal curve**

10 know how to solve problems for Normal variables by converting to standardised variables (z-scores)

11 know the notation for a Normal variable X, i.e.

$$X \sim N(\mu, \sigma^2)$$

where μ is the mean value of X and σ is the standard deviation of X.

4 Data collection

A Data, data everywhere! (answers p. 113)

The collection, analysis and interpretation of information have a very high public profile. The following three examples of statistical articles are taken from a national newspaper on a single day.

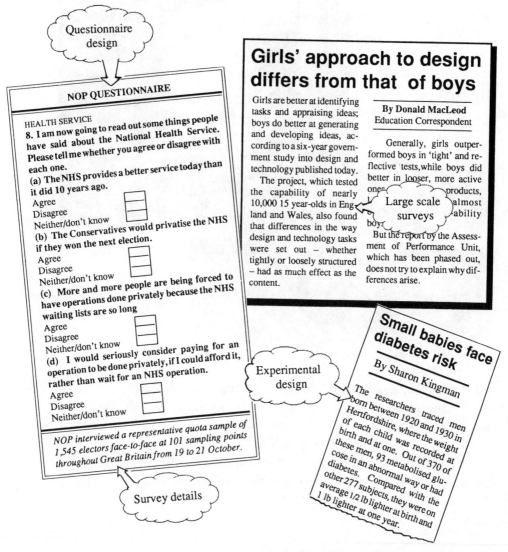

The Independent, 25 October 1991

Survey or experiment

There are two ways in which data may be collected in response to a particular problem, by **survey** or by **experiment**.

In a survey, information is gathered under existing conditions in an attempt to determine some particular characteristic(s) of a population.

In an experiment, comparisons are made between two or more groups under strictly controlled conditions where the factor that is being tested is the only variable. A trial to ascertain the effectiveness of a particular drug is a good example of an experiment.

1D	A biology class proposes to investigate the effect of water temperature on the growth rate of tadpoles. They have 150 tadpoles, together with a number of jars with thermostats, and have decided to compare temperatures of 10°C, 15°C and 20°C.
	Discuss the design of this investigation and consider general ideas that might be useful in the design of other investigations.

The key differences between surveys and experiments are summarised below.

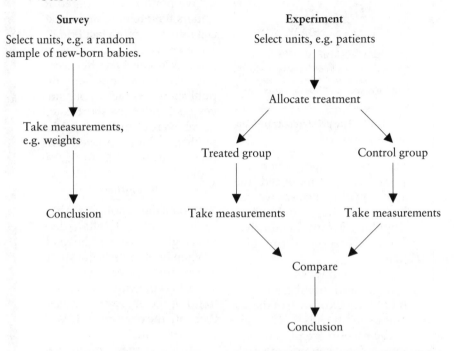

Survey

Select units, e.g. a random sample of new-born babies.

Take measurements, e.g. weights

Conclusion

Experiment

Select units, e.g. patients

Allocate treatment

Treated group   Control group

Take measurements   Take measurements

Compare

Conclusion

2D   Suppose you are to investigate whether the weight of a new-born baby is likely to be affected if the mother smokes during pregnancy.

Discuss the advantages of doing this by these means.

(a) Collecting appropriate data from a survey

(b) Setting up an experiment

B Survey methods (answers p. 114)

You need to be careful about *how* you collect information. For example, a potentially embarrassing question may not produce an honest response. A national newspaper, in an attempt to find out if people actually read the books they buy, proceeded as outlined in the article below.

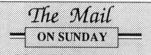

ON SUNDAY

READERSHIP SURVEY

If you find this leaflet while reading this book, please contact the Mail on Sunday If you do so before Friday October 25, 1991, we will pay you £5

SURVEY: The printed note hidden inside 240 novels

Four weeks ago, when the Booker jury announced the short-list of six novels, we visited book shops in London, Brighton, Oxford, Cambridge, Stratford-upon-Avon and Bath.

We secretly slid a small printed and numbered note into 40 copies of each of the six nominated novels – 240 in all.

The notes were placed two-thirds of the way through each book, jammed hard against the spine so they could not be shaken out, yet were impossible to miss by anyone who actually opened that particular page.

Five pounds was offered to finders who telephoned a special number before last Friday.

We know all the books were sold. We checked this week with the bookshops and the publishers. At each of our survey bookshops the short-listed novels were re-ordered and the publishers had reprinted runs ranging from 6,000 to 15,000 copies.

Response

Yet, come the deadline, we had received only 19 calls – less than eight per cent of the total.

When NOP inserts questionnaires into magazines, with almost no incentive to readers to fill in the answers and post them off, the response rate is 20 to 30 per cent.

And the survey sample was not too small to draw conclusions. After all, elections have been timed on national surveys of only 1,000 people.

The Mail on Sunday, 27 October 1991

1 Comment on the 'design' of this survey.

This section aims to help you think about the *collection* of data – deciding exactly *what* data you need and *how* to go about collecting it. No amount of clever analysis can make up for inadequate data collection.

Conducting a survey is a commonly used method of obtaining information about a population. So that you do not have to count or measure *every* member, it is usual to obtain information from a *sample* of the population.

A survey provides information about a population from a sample of the population.

To ensure that there is no selection bias, each member of the sample is usually chosen by a random process. Even when the sample is selected correctly, other factors are important in ensuring that the data provide representative information about a population.

2D A town planning department wishes to use a survey to discover what facilities may be required in a sports centre they intend to build. Describe how they might obtain the information and any problems they may encounter in ensuring that they have representative views of those living in the town.

We will consider some aspects of sampling methods by looking at an example of a forest survey.

Forest plantations cover 10% of the total land area of Great Britain – more than 2.1 million hectares. Almost half of this area is owned by the Forestry Commission and the remainder by private owners, ranging from individuals to large estates and companies. The management of these plantations requires good estimates of the quantity and quality of timber involved.

Suppose a forest plot, consisting of pine trees of the same age, is to be sold.

Suppose further that you need to estimate the number of trees standing on the plot and the proportion which may be classified as large.

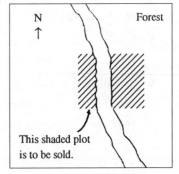

N ↑   Forest

This shaded plot is to be sold.

Assuming that there are too many trees to count individually, the plot might be divided into a number of sampling areas. Suppose that there are 72 such areas on the west side of a river and another 96 on the east side. Information is collected from 14 of the areas.

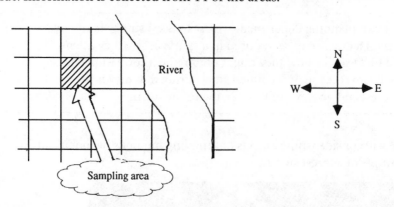

3D   (a)   What information do you need to collect from each area? What practical problems may need to be overcome when collecting such information?

(b)   Will 14 of the areas prove sufficient for the sample?

You will need a means of generating random numbers. The tables on pages 53 and 54 provide the necessary information on the trees in 168 areas of the forest, each area being a five-hectare rectangle.

The task is to estimate the total number of trees on the plot being sold and the proportion of large trees on the plot.

Sampling 14 of the areas will be sufficient.

Two different **sampling schemes** are proposed – schemes A and B. Conduct the survey using one scheme, then the other.

Sampling scheme A: select 14 areas at random from the 168 on the plot

4   How can you select 14 numbers from 1 to 168 inclusive? Is your method efficient?

5   Devise a suitable table for recording your results. Select the areas and record the appropriate data.

6   Calculate the means for the 14 areas. Hence estimate these.

(a)   The numbers of trees on the plot

(b)   The number of large trees on the plot

(c)   The proportion of large trees on the plot

Sampling scheme B: select 6 areas at random from the west of the river (region 1) and 8 from the east (region 2)

7 Why do you think the numbers 6 and 8 have been used?

8 Devise a suitable means of selecting the areas and a table for recording your results. Results for the two regions should be kept separate.

9 Calculate the means of your results from each region. Hence estimate the proportion of large trees on the plot.

10 Calculate the variances of the total number of trees per area in each of your two samples. Suggest why choosing a stratified sample of 14 areas with more than 8 from region 2 might have improved the reliability of your estimates.

Sampling scheme A used a **simple random sample**. Scheme B used a **stratified random sample**, so called because the plot was divided into two regions (strata) which might be expected to have different growing conditions.

Region 1

Area	Small	Large	Total	Area	Small	Large	Total	Area	Small	Large	Total
1	97	142	239	25	75	128	203	49	92	136	228
2	77	113	190	26	87	117	204	50	86	123	209
3	75	126	201	27	71	121	192	51	91	135	226
4	91	165	256	28	107	142	249	52	92	125	217
5	92	136	228	29	90	148	238	53	92	131	223
6	77	106	183	30	78	113	191	54	89	121	210
7	106	143	249	31	88	131	219	55	91	123	214
8	83	143	226	32	107	147	254	56	89	144	233
9	86	135	221	33	83	126	209	57	94	136	230
10	99	142	241	34	79	111	190	58	77	132	209
11	69	107	176	35	77	125	202	59	84	125	209
12	92	149	241	36	95	145	240	60	85	136	221
13	88	133	221	37	77	112	189	61	82	121	203
14	92	132	224	38	74	114	188	62	90	138	228
15	74	127	201	39	93	153	246	63	86	128	214
16	78	135	213	40	85	137	222	64	77	116	193
17	92	135	227	41	95	144	239	65	88	111	199
18	75	120	195	42	94	142	236	66	110	146	256
19	97	137	234	43	79	131	210	67	88	146	234
20	84	126	210	44	80	118	198	68	84	143	227
21	87	128	215	45	84	114	198	69	91	139	230
22	87	138	225	46	80	127	207	70	81	124	205
23	87	134	221	47	105	158	263	71	79	123	202
24	87	134	221	48	76	122	198	72	93	149	242

Region 2

Area	Small	Large	Total	Area	Small	Large	Total	Area	Small	Large	Total
73	114	232	346	105	97	208	305	137	105	186	291
74	91	189	280	106	93	186	279	138	130	240	370
75	86	209	295	107	89	207	296	139	100	240	340
76	101	268	369	108	110	238	348	140	96	234	330
77	108	224	332	109	91	186	277	141	105	228	333
78	92	177	269	110	86	190	276	142	94	206	300
79	125	234	359	111	107	249	356	143	92	203	295
80	95	233	328	112	98	225	323	144	107	243	350
81	100	222	322	113	110	236	346	145	106	217	323
82	116	233	349	114	109	232	341	146	104	224	328
83	81	179	260	115	91	215	306	147	111	256	367
84	106	242	348	116	94	196	290	148	100	232	332
85	102	220	322	117	101	189	290	149	136	270	406
86	108	218	326	118	92	210	302	150	77	162	239
87	85	209	294	119	121	258	379	151	126	239	365
88	90	221	311	120	88	202	290	152	102	239	341
89	107	222	329	121	107	224	331	153	112	255	367
90	87	199	286	122	101	204	305	154	100	211	311
91	113	226	339	123	106	222	328	155	93	196	289
92	99	208	307	124	110	207	317	156	121	239	360
93	102	211	313	125	109	216	325	157	107	253	360
94	101	226	327	126	106	200	306	158	100	226	326
95	101	221	322	127	107	205	312	159	104	218	322
96	102	220	322	128	102	236	338	160	98	241	339
97	86	211	297	129	110	224	334	161	90	201	291
98	103	195	298	130	88	217	305	162	86	207	293
99	83	199	282	131	99	207	306	163	94	196	290
100	126	234	360	132	98	224	322	164	88	201	289
101	103	242	345	133	97	199	296	165	118	256	374
102	92	189	281	134	105	226	331	166	104	189	293
103	104	215	319	135	101	211	312	167	107	238	345
104	125	241	366	136	90	193	283	168	103	241	344

A **simple random sample** is one where every member of the
population has an equal chance of being selected.

For a population made up of a number of sub-groups, or **strata**, a
stratified sample is one where each stratum is sampled separately.
In the simplest form of stratified sample, the number chosen from
each stratum is proportional to the size of that stratum.

If an estimate produced by one sampling scheme is likely to be better than that produced by another, then the first scheme is said to have greater **precision**.

One way to improve the precision of a scheme is simply to increase the size of the sample. However, a larger sample involves greater time and cost and so other methods of improving precision are preferred.

> A good sampling scheme is one which achieves precision from relatively small samples.

Using stratified sampling to improve precision

Suppose that the aces are removed from an ordinary pack of cards and that the remaining cards are assigned scores as follows.

2	3	4	5	6	7	8	9	10	J	Q	K
2	3	4	5	6	7	8	9	10	10	10	10

The mean score is then $\dfrac{2 + \ldots + 9 + 4 \times 10}{12} = 7$. Knowing the actual mean score allows you to see how well various sampling schemes estimate this mean.

11 Shuffle the pack and take two cards at random. Calculate the mean of your sample. This will be an estimate of the actual mean score, 7.

12 Replacing the cards between samples, repeat the method used in question 11 until you have twenty estimates of the actual mean score. Plot a simple stick graph of these estimates like the example below.

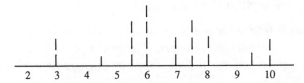

13 Now suppose the pack is split into two, with all the cards which score 7 or less in one pack (stratum) and all the cards of score more than 7 in the other pack. Shuffle each pack and select one card from each pack. Calculate the mean of your sample of two cards.

14 Repeat the sampling method used in question 13 until you have twenty estimates of the actual mean score. Compare a simple stick graph of these estimates with the one obtained in question 12. Which sampling method appears to have greater precision?

15E   Use a computer or calculator to investigate the effect of choosing samples of greater size and of choosing stratified samples which sample the cards up to 7 more intensely than the higher value cards.

To improve precision using stratified sampling, the stratification chosen should split the population into groups whose means are as different as possible.

16D | Describe how you might choose the strata in a survey to estimate the amount of money per week spent on entertainment by 16–19-year-olds.

It is not necessary to sample each stratum equally. If one of the strata is very variable and another more uniform, then you should ensure that a thorough sample is taken of the more variable stratum.

17D | Suppose you have to predict the support for the various political parties in a forthcoming general election. Suppose further that the electorate has been divided into strata according to age and profession. Explain why it might be appropriate to sample more heavily from the young and from white collar workers.

In surveys of people's opinions it is usually not practicable to seek a true random sample within each stratum. Instead, an approach called **quota sampling** is used. Each interviewer is told how many men and women to question, as well as how many from each age group and social class. It is then left to the interviewers to choose the actual individuals they will question.

C Questionnaire design (answers p. 117)

The National Food Survey was introduced during the Second World War and is still carried out each year. A large sample of householders are asked to record how much food they buy during one week and how much it costs.

In large surveys of this type it is impractical to interview participants and so a questionnaire is used instead. Many design features of a 'good' questionnaire are simply common sense.

- It is crucial to define exactly what it is that you want to measure. You should avoid asking unnecessary questions and gathering information which cannot be used. In addition you do not want the questionnaire to be so long that it puts people off!

- Each question must be worded so that it is easy to understand and unambiguous. This is especially important if respondents have to fill in the questionnaire themselves.

- If a question is sensitive, then it has to be asked particularly carefully so as not to give offence. Sensitive questions should be avoided at the beginning of the questionnaire.
- Each question should be formulated in an unbiased way.
- It is usually best to start with easy questions. Think of a logical order from one topic to the next. Start each topic with general questions and then go on to more specific ones.
- Before a questionnaire is used in a large-scale study, it should be tested in a 'pilot study'.

| 1D | Describe how some of the above design features are applied in the following extract from a questionnaire on milk consumption. |

Milk questionnaire

We are undertaking some research to find out how we can improve our service to you. Your help in completing this questionnaire would be very much appreciated.

Please read through each question and answer each one by ticking or filling in the box corresponding with your reply.

Q1 How many members of your household are there ?

    1 ☐   2 ☐   3 ☐   4 ☐   5 or more ☐

Q2 In an average week where do you buy milk?

    Doorstep delivery ☐   Supermarket ☐   (Tick one or
    Small shop   ☐   Farm   ☐   more boxes)
    Other (please specify) ☐ ....

Q3 In an average week does your household buy semi-skimmed milk?

    Yes ☐   No ☐

If you answered yes please answer questions 4 and 5. Otherwise proceed to question 6.

Q4 In an average week how many pints of semi-skimmed milk does your household buy ? ☐

Some questions are **closed response** questions. The respondent has to choose one or more answers from a list or give a rating on a scale which is provided.

Other questions are **open response**. Respondents are not restricted in their answers.

2D

(a) What would be an open response question format for question 2 in the milk questionnaire?

(b) Suggest some of the advantages and disadvantages of open response questions. What are the advantages and disadvantages of closed response questions?

(c) Discuss the actual format of question 2 in the light of your answers to part (b).

One of the main problems with questionnaires concerns the fact that bias may be introduced because of major differences between those who return a completed questionnaire and those who do not. This problem can be partially offset by selecting from the completed forms a fixed number of forms for various strata that have previously been defined.

An alternative to the use of questionnaires is telephone sampling.

3D

Describe some of the advantages and disadvantages of telephone sampling.

After working through this chapter you should

1   be more aware of potential problems when collecting data and, in particular, know that you should always define properly what you want to measure

2   know that statistical information may be collected either by surveys or experiments and be aware of the differences between these methods

3   understand the terms random sample and stratified sample

4   know what is meant by the precision of a sampling scheme

5   understand some of the advantages of stratified surveys.

5 From binomial to Normal

A Finding probabilities (answers p. 117)

In Chapter 1 you met the binomial distribution, an important model for a *discrete* random variable under certain conditions. For example, the binomial probability distribution for the number of heads when 30 coins are thrown is shown below.

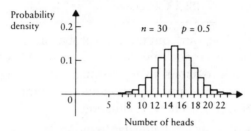

1 What other distribution does this remind you of?

2D | Use a spreadsheet simulation (for example the 'Binomial distributions' worksheet in the BINO.XLS file of the DISCUS package) to investigate for what values of n and p you will obtain an approximately bell-shaped curve. (See page iv for information about DISCUS.)

Although there are obvious similarities between some binomial distributions and the Normal curve, there are complications, not least of which is the fact that the Normal distribution models a **continuous** variable, while the binomial distribution is for a **discrete** variable.

3D | What is the difference between a **discrete** and a **continuous** random variable?

You will have seen from question 2D that:

> The binomial distribution is bell-shaped for values of p close to $\frac{1}{2}$, even for quite low values of n.
>
> Even for p not close to $\frac{1}{2}$ the distribution is bell-shaped for larger values of n.

It is difficult to calculate the probabilities of some events using the binomial model.

4D

> (a) A box contains 60 dice. A prize of a car is offered to anyone who obtains 30 or more sixes on turning out the dice from the box. It is worth paying 10p for a turn?
>
> (b) Would it be worth paying 10p if the prize were £10 for 20 or more sixes?
>
> (Questions of these kinds could be investigated with a spreadsheet simulation, such as the 'Binomial distributions' worksheet in the BINO.XLS file of the DISCUS package.)

You could, in principle, work out the exact probabilities of these events using a binomial model, although to do so would be very difficult. It is possible to obtain an approximate result using the Normal distribution as an approximation to the binomial distribution. For example, consider the following situation.

If the probability of being left-handed is found to be 0.1, what is the probability that there will be 60 left-handed children in a school of 500 children?

Let X be the number of left-handed children.
X will have binomial distribution with $p = 0.1$, $n = 500$.
It is convenient to write this as:

$$X \sim B(500, 0.1)$$

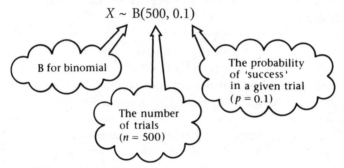

The probability of there being *exactly* 60 left-handers is

$$\binom{500}{60}(0.1)^{60}(0.9)^{440}$$

To work out $\binom{500}{60}$ you would need a very large number of rows of Pascal's triangle and the numbers would be too large for a calculator. It would be even more difficult to calculate the probability of 60 *or more*.

$$P(60 \text{ or more}) = P(60) + P(61) + P(62) + \ldots + P(500)$$

The similarity with the Normal distribution may provide an alternative basis for the calculation, since using Normal tables to obtain probabilities is relatively easy.

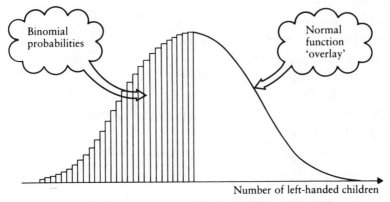

Number of left-handed children

The distribution looks very close to the bell-shaped Normal distribution. In order to obtain the right Normal curve to describe this situation you need to know the mean and variance of the binomial distribution B(500, 0.1).

The mean and variance of the binomial distribution

If a Normal distribution is used as an approximation to a binomial distribution then the Normal and the binomial distribution should have the same mean and variance.

5 Use a computer simulation (such as the 'Binomial distributions' worksheet in the BINO.XLS file of DISCUS) to obtain the mean, variance and standard deviation for a variety of binomial distributions. Use your results to copy and complete this table.

n	p	Mean (of B(n, p))	Variance (of B(n, p))	Standard deviation (of B(n, p))
10	$\frac{1}{2}$			
20	$\frac{1}{2}$			
20	$\frac{1}{4}$			
40	$\frac{1}{2}$			
40	$\frac{1}{4}$			
100	$\frac{1}{2}$			

6 Find a formula for the mean in terms of n and p.

7 Find a formula for the variance in terms of n and p.

8 Find a formula for standard deviation in terms of n and p.

If a binomial variable is to be modelled by a Normal variable then the Normal variable must have the *same* mean and the *same* variance.

The mean of $B(n, p)$ is np.
The variance of $B(n, p)$ is $np(1 - p)$.
Given $q = 1 - p$ then $np(1 - p) = npq$.

A binomial model and its Normal approximation should have the same mean and the same variance. If

$$X \sim B(n, p)$$

is approximated by

$$Y \sim N(\mu, \sigma^2)$$

then $\mu = np$, and $\sigma^2 = npq$.

You can use this information to solve the original problem. It can be done approximately as follows.

The number of left-handed children $X \sim B(500, 0.1)$.
A Normal variable Y with mean $= np = 50$ and standard deviation $= \sqrt{npq} \approx 6.7$ would model this distribution.

60 is about $1\frac{1}{2}$ standard deviations above the mean, i.e. the standardised value is approximately 1.5.

$$\Phi(1.5) = 0.9332 \qquad \text{(from tables)}$$

So there is only about a 7% probability that there will be more than 60 left-handed children in the school.

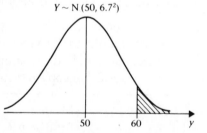

$Y \sim N(50, 6.7^2)$

9 Make a similar approximate calculation to show that when 1000 coins are thrown it is likely that between 470 and 530 heads will be obtained.

You have seen that, in certain situations, although the binomial distribution really applies it is often more convenient to use the Normal distribution as an approximation. This is particularly true when n is large, when the calculation of binomial probabilities would be very tedious. This approach is illustrated in the following example.

Suppose a student takes a test composed of 48 multiple-choice questions. Each question has four possible answers of which only one is correct. The student is unable to answer any of the questions, so she guesses. Find the probability that she will obtain a pass mark by getting 20 or more correct answers.

X = number of correct guesses

$X \sim B(48, \frac{1}{4})$

Before tackling a problem, define clearly the random variable . . .

To solve the problem, you need $P(X \geqslant 20)$.

. . . and its distribution.

10 What Normal distribution would you use to approximate $B(48, \frac{1}{4})$?

To find the required probability (of 20 *or more* correct guesses) you must take into account the fact that you are using a continuous distribution (Normal) as an approximation to a discrete distribution (binomial). The diagram below shows the right-hand side of the correct binomial distribution.

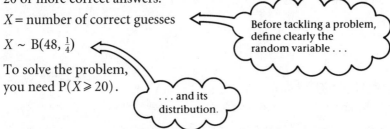

The shaded area represents the probability of 20 or more correct guesses

20
19.5   20.5   Number correct

On the binomial model,
$$P(X \geqslant 20) = P(X = 20) + P(X = 21) + \ldots + P(X = 48).$$
This probability is represented by the shaded columns on the distribution.

You can model the distribution of $X \sim B(48, \frac{1}{4})$ with the distribution of a Normal random variable, Y, where $Y \sim N(12, 9)$.

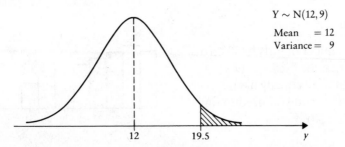

$Y \sim N(12, 9)$

Mean $= 12$
Variance $= 9$

12   19.5 y

When $X \sim B(48, \frac{1}{4})$ then $P(X \geqslant 20)$ is approximately the same as $P(Y > 19.5)$ when $Y \sim N(12, 9)$.

The probability for $X \geqslant 20$ is therefore the area to the right of 19.5 on the appropriate Normal distribution. The relevant area is shaded on the diagram at the foot of page 63.

The standardised value, z, is given by $z = \dfrac{y - \mu}{\sigma}$.

For $y = 19.5$

$$z = \frac{19.5 - 12}{3} = 2.5$$

The area to the *left* of z is

$$\Phi(2.5) = 0.994 \quad \text{(to 3 s.f.)}$$

11 Why is the area to the *right* of $z = 2.5$,

$$1 - 0.994 = 0.006?$$

The probability of a pass using guesswork alone is therefore less than 1%.

When the Normal distribution approximates closely to the binomial

You have seen that the binomial distribution is bell-shaped when p is close to $\frac{1}{2}$ even for quite low values of n and that it becomes bell-shaped for large values of n even when p is not very close to $\frac{1}{2}$.

As a rough guide:

> The Normal distribution is a reasonably good approximation to the Binomial distribution $B(n, p)$ when $n \geqslant 30$ *and* $np \geqslant 5$.

Clearly these values can be adjusted upwards if a very accurate probability is required or downwards if a very rough idea of probability will do.

Example 1

Find the probability that *between* 25 and 30 of the next 50 births at a hospital will be of girls.

Solution

Let $x = $ number of girls in 50 births. *Assume* that the births of boys and of girls are equally likely. $X \sim B(50, \frac{1}{2})$ and you need to find $P(25 < X < 30)$.

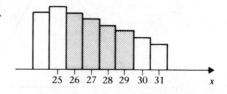

The variable $Y \sim N(25, 3.54^2)$ is an appropriate model for the distribution of X.

You require $P(25.5 < Y < 29.5)$.

Standardizing, $\quad z_1 = \dfrac{29.5 - 25}{3.54} = 1.27$

$$z_2 = \dfrac{25.5 - 25}{3.54} = 0.14$$

$$P(25 < X < 30) = \Phi(1.27) - \Phi(0.14)$$

$$= 0.8980 - 0.5557$$

$$= 0.342 \text{ (to 3 s.f.)}$$

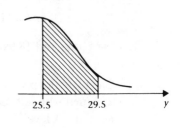

Exercise A (answers p. 119)

1 A coin is tossed a number of times. Using an appropriate Normal approximation, calculate approximately these probabilities.

(a) 52 or more heads in 100 tosses

(b) 520 or more heads in 1000 tosses

(c) 5200 or more heads in 10 000 tosses

2 From experience, an employer finds that he has to reject 30% of applicants as unsatisfactory for employment as machine operatives. What is the probability that after interviewing 200 applicants he will find at least 150 who are suitable for work in his new factory?

3 Thirty dice are thrown. Find the probability of obtaining exactly 5 ones.

4 It is known that 2% of all light bulbs are faulty. What is the probability that there will be more than 20 faulty bulbs in a consignment of 1000?

5 15% of the biscuits produced by a particular machine are misshapen. What is the probability of these events in a batch of 1000 biscuits?

(a) Fewer than 130 are misshapen.

(b) Between 140 and 155, exclusive, are misshapen.

6 A gardener sows 75 sunflower seeds in his allotment. The packet states that 80% of the seeds will germinate. What is the probability that more than 65 seeds will germinate?

7 In Eastfork, 24% of the population have blood type Y. If 250 blood donors are taken at random what is the probability that fewer than 55 will be of blood type Y?

8 A coin is biased so that the probability that it will land heads up is $\frac{3}{5}$. The coin is thrown 160 times. Find the probability that there will be *between* 90 and 100 heads.

9   In 1984, 11% of households in Britain owned a microwave oven. If a random sample of 200 households were interviewed, work out these probabilities.

   (a) Fewer than 20 owned a microwave oven

   (b) Between 20 and 30 households owned a microwave oven

10   18.6% of boys and 18.9% of girls leaving school in 1987 had at least one A level.

   (a) Calculate the probability of finding, in a random sample of 250 men who left school in 1987, more than 50 who have at least one A level.

   (b) If 300 women (who left school in 1987) were interviewed, find the probability that between 50 and 60 had at least one A level.

After working through this chapter you should

1   understand that the Normal distribution can be used as a model for the binomial in some circumstances and that this provides an easy way of estimating binomial probabilities

2   know that the Normal distribution is a good approximation to $B(n, p)$ if p is close to $\frac{1}{2}$ and that, if p is not very close to $\frac{1}{2}$, large values of n are necessary before a Normal distribution can closely fit the particular binomial model (as a guide, when $n \geqslant 30$ and $np \geqslant 5$)

3   know that if $X \sim B(n, p)$ then

   $$\text{mean of } X = np, \qquad \text{variance of } X = npq$$

4   know that if $B(n, p)$ is approximated by $N(\mu, \sigma^2)$ then

   $$\mu = np, \qquad \sigma^2 = npq$$

5   be able to use the Normal approximation to the binomial distribution to solve problems.

6 Estimating population parameters

A Sampling distribution of the mean (answers p. 120)

A manufacturer of slot machines decides to check for invalid coins by incorporating a weighing device into each machine. Checking coins is not straightforward since there is considerable variation of the weights of genuine coins. The problem is to decide what **weight range** the machines should accept.

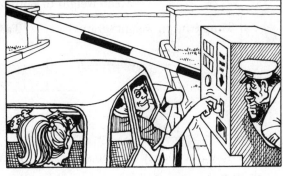

It is not possible to weigh all the coins in circulation in an attempt to find acceptable weight limits. Taking a **sample** of coins is possible but the problem is how to relate information from the sample to the population.

These are the weights in grams of 100 2p coins used in Chapter 3.

7.15	7.08	7.09	7.05	7.33
7.05	7.09	7.12	7.18	7.19
7.08	7.09	7.09	7.20	7.07
7.12	7.11	7.26	6.86	7.14
6.80	7.11	6.99	7.05	7.11
7.27	6.97	7.40	7.12	7.44
7.17	7.17	7.05	7.18	7.13
7.11	7.19	7.16	7.04	7.15
7.11	7.01	7.21	7.02	7.05
7.03	7.22	7.30	7.18	7.14
7.08	7.06	7.30	7.12	7.04
7.11	7.16	7.07	7.22	7.18
7.24	7.20	7.09	7.13	7.11
6.95	7.01	7.18	7.23	7.16
7.00	7.08	7.03	7.04	7.18
7.17	7.12	7.14	7.13	7.18
7.19	7.07	6.98	7.22	7.15
7.34	7.18	7.21	7.06	7.24
6.98	7.25	7.19	7.29	7.17
7.20	7.04	7.17	7.19	7.11

You know that the distribution of the weights, W, is Normal (or approximately Normal) and their mean, $\overline{w}$, is 7.13 g and their variance is 0.01.

1   Use two-figure random numbers from a calculator, computer or tables to take at least 50 samples of size 2 from this population. (The coins can be selected more than once.) Calculate the mean of each sample and record your results in a table like this.

Mean weight of samples of size 2

Sample mean weight (grams)	Tally	Frequency
6.80–		
6.85–		
6.90–		
6.95–		

2   Draw a frequency chart to show the distribution of the sample means.

3   Calculate the mean and variance of the distribution of the sample means.

4   Comment on the similarities and differences between the parent population and the distribution of the sample means.

It is clear that a large number of possible samples may be selected from a population. If, for each sample, the mean is calculated and the distribution of mean values is plotted, you obtain the **sampling distribution of the mean**.

In the work on coins you should have noticed these things:

> The distribution of the sample means looks like a Normal distribution.
>
> The distribution of the sample means has the same mean as the parent population.

It is noticeable that the distribution of the sample means is more tightly clustered around the mean than is the parent population. This is borne out by the fact that its variance is smaller than the variance of the parent population.

You will need to investigate further to discover whether the variance of the distribution of the sample means is related in some way to the variance of the parent population.

5   Use software which allows sampling from a Normal population with mean $\mu = 0$ and variance $\sigma^2 = 1$ (for example, the 'Samples (normal pop)' worksheet in the SAMP.XLS file of the DISCUS package) to take about 10 samples of size 4. Record the mean and standard deviation of your sample each time in a table.

(a) What do you notice about your means?

(b) What do you notice about your standard deviations?

6 Repeat question 5 for samples of size 8, 10 and 20.

7 What happens to your means as the sample size increases? What happens to your standard deviations as the sample size increases?

8 Using software which will take a large number of small samples (for example, the 'Means (normal pop)' worksheet in the SAMP.XLS file of DISCUS) take 100 samples of size 4.

Note down the **mean of the sample means** and the **standard deviation of the sample means**. Square this to get the **variance of the sample means**.

9 Repeat question 8 for sample sizes 8, 10 and 20.

10 Plot a graph of variance against $\dfrac{1}{\text{sample size}}$. What do you notice?

11 Check that the variance in each case is approximately $\dfrac{1}{n}$.

Remember that in this case the parent population had a mean of 0 and variance of 1.

In general if the parent population is distributed $N(\mu, \sigma^2)$ and samples of size n are taken,

- the distribution of the sample means is Normal
- the mean of the distribution of the sample means is equal to the mean of the parent population
- the larger the sample size, the more tightly clustered around its mean is the distribution (i.e. the smaller is the variance of the distribution of the sample means)
- if the population variance is σ^2 and samples of size n are taken, then the distribution of the sample means of these samples will have variance $\dfrac{\sigma^2}{n}$.

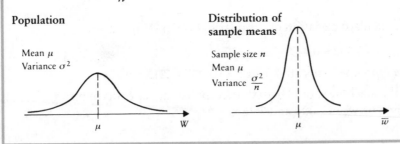

Population

Mean μ
Variance σ^2

Distribution of sample means

Sample size n
Mean μ
Variance $\dfrac{\sigma^2}{n}$

You should now have a good idea of how the distribution of the sample mean is related to that of its parent population.

It is now possible to consider how an acceptable weight interval for the coin checking machine on p. 67 might be chosen.

Assume that the distribution of the weights of all 2p coins in circulation is Normal with mean 7.13 g and variance of $0.01\,\text{g}^2$.

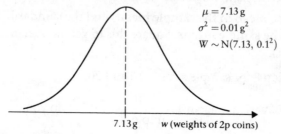

$$\mu = 7.13\,\text{g}$$
$$\sigma^2 = 0.01\,\text{g}^2$$
$$W \sim N(7.13,\ 0.1^2)$$

7.13 g   w (weights of 2p coins)

Suppose the machine is fed 5 coins, each 2p, and records the mean weight.

The distribution of the mean weight of samples of 5 coins will:

- be Normal

- have mean $\mu = 7.13$ g

- have variance $\dfrac{\sigma^2}{n} = \dfrac{0.01}{5}$
$$= 0.002$$

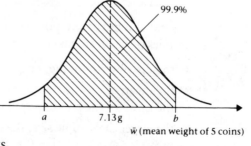

99.9%

a   7.13 g   b

w̄ (mean weight of 5 coins)

Suppose the acceptance limits a and b are such that the machine accepts 99.9% of all batches of 5 coins.

The limits to include 99.9% of all coins will be very close to 3 standard deviations either side of the mean.

12D | Check this using Normal tables.

The standard deviation of the distribution of sample means is
$$\sqrt{0.002} = 0.447$$

Therefore the limits are $7.13 \pm 3 \times 0.0447 = 7.13 \pm 0.134$.

So the machine should be set to accept batches of coins of mean weight between 7.00 g and 7.26 g.

Sampling from other distributions – The Central Limit Theorem

You have been sampling from a parent population which you know is Normal. It is interesting to consider the distribution of the sample means when other kinds of parent population are sampled.

13 Using software (such as the 'Means (uniform pop)' worksheet in the SAMP.XLS file of the DISCUS package) that allows sampling from a uniform distribution, take 100 samples of size 4.

Record the **mean of the sample means** and the **standard deviation of the sample means**. Square this for the **variance of the sample means**.

Note down also the mean, standard deviation and variance of the distribution that you were using.

14 Repeat question 13 for samples of size 8, 10 and 20.

15 Plot a graph of variance against $\dfrac{1}{\text{sample size}}$. What do you notice?

16 Check that the variance in each case is *approximately* $\dfrac{\sigma^2}{n}$ (where σ^2 is the original population variance).

17 Repeat questions 13 to 16 for an exponential distribution (using software such as the 'Means (exponential pop)' worksheet in the SAMP.XLS file of the DISCUS package) or for any other distribution.

You should have noticed the following.

> If the sample size is large enough then the distribution of the sample means is *approximately* Normal, irrespective of the distribution of the parent population.
>
> The mean of the distribution of the sample means is approximately equal to the mean of the parent population.
>
> The variance of the distribution of the sample means is approximately the variance of the parent population divided by the sample size.
>
> These approximations get closer as the sample size gets bigger.
>
> These important results are known as the **Central Limit Theorem**.
>
> Symbolically if $X \sim (\text{unknown})(\mu, \sigma^2)$ then $\overline{X}_n \sim \mathrm{N}\left(\mu, \dfrac{\sigma^2}{n}\right)$
>
> provided n is sufficiently large. (A good rule of thumb is $n \geqslant 30$.)

The Central Limit Theorem is crucial to work on sampling. It enables you to make predictions about the distribution of the sample mean even if you do not know the distribution of the parent population. In addition you can be confident that the mean of the sample is close to the population mean, provided the sample is large enough.

The Central Limit Theorem can be proved, but this is beyond the scope of work at this level.

Example 1

The mean weight of trout in a fish farm is 980 g and the standard deviation is 100 g. What is the probability that a catch of 10 trout will have a mean weight per fish of more than 1050 g?

Solution

Assume that the distribution of weight of the population (of all fish in the farm) is $N(980, 100^2)$.

Parent population

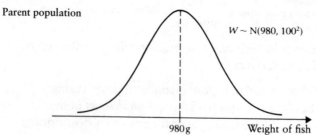

$W \sim N(980, 100^2)$

980 g   Weight of fish

The catch of 10 fish is a sample of size $n = 10$. The mean weight of samples of 10:

- is distributed Normally
- has a mean of 980 g
- has a variance of $\dfrac{100^2}{10} = 1000 = 31.6^2$.

Distribution of the sample means
$(n = 10)$

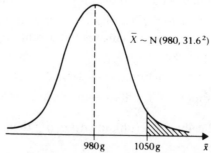

$\bar{X} \sim N(980, 31.6^2)$

980 g   1050 g $\bar{x}$

The probability of obtaining a sample of 10 having a mean weight per fish greater than 1050 g is represented by the shaded area on the sketch of the distribution.

Standardising the weight of 1050 g gives

$$z = \frac{1050 - 980}{\sqrt{1000}} = 2.21$$

$$P(Z > 2.21) = 1 - \Phi(2.21)$$

$$= 1 - 0.9864 \quad \text{(from Normal tables – see p. 40)}$$

$$= 0.0136$$

So the probability of obtaining a sample mean weight greater than 1050 g is 0.0136.

In other words, about 1.4% of all samples of 10 will have a mean weight per fish greater than 1050 g.

Example 2

Screws are produced with a mean length of 4 cm and standard deviation 0.2 cm.

How large a sample should be taken to be 95% certain that the mean of the sample will be within 0.1 cm of the population mean length?

Solution

Let L represent the distribution of the lengths, l.

Let the required sample size be n.

Population

$\sigma^2 = 0.2^2$
$\mu = 4.0$

4.0 l(cm)

Distribution of sample means (size n)

Variance $= \dfrac{\sigma^2}{n} = \dfrac{0.2^2}{n}$

Mean $= 4.0$

3.9   4.0   4.1 $\bar{l}$(cm)

So $L \sim N(4.0, 0.2^2)$ and $\bar{L} \sim N\left(4.0, \dfrac{0.2^2}{n}\right)$

You require

$$P(3.9 < \bar{L} < 4.1) = 0.95$$

This is represented by the shaded area shown.

Consider the upper end of the distribution of sample means.

$z = 1.96$ (from tables)

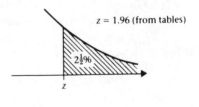

$2\frac{1}{2}\%$

z

$$1.96 = \frac{4.1 - 4.0}{0.2/\sqrt{n}}$$

$$\Rightarrow \sqrt{n} = \frac{1.96 \times 0.2}{0.1}$$

$$n = 15.4 \quad \text{(to 3 s.f.)}$$

To be 95% certain of a sample with mean screw length between 3.9 and 4.1 cm you should take 16 screws.

Exercise A (answers p. 121)

1   The girls of sixth-form age in a large town have a mean height of 166 cm and standard deviation 6 cm.

In one school there is a mathematics group with 5 girls. What is the probability that the mean height of this group is in the interval (162 cm, 170 cm)?

There are 8 girls in an English group. What is the probability that the mean height of the English group lies in the interval (162 cm, 170 cm)?

2   The mean weight of trout in a fish farm is 980 g. The standard deviation of the weights is 120 g.

If 10 fish are caught at random what are the probabilities that the mean weight of the catch is in these intervals?

(a) (970 g, 1010 g)   (b) (950 g, 1030 g)   (c) (940 g, 1040 g)

3   Boys aged 13 in a large town have a mean height of 162 cm and standard deviation 3.5 cm.

What size sample of boys must be taken, to be 95% certain that the mean height of the sample will be in these intervals?

(a) 160.5 cm to 163.5 cm   (b) 161 cm to 163 cm?

4   The mean length of a mass-produced metal rod is 7.3 cm. The standard deviation of the lengths is 0.078 cm.

What size sample must be taken, to be 95% certain that the mean length of the sample will be in these intervals?

(a) (7.27 cm, 7.33 cm)   (b) (7.29 cm, 7.31 cm)

5   A packaging machine produces packets of butter with a mean weight of 250 g and standard deviation 5 g. If 10 packets are chosen at random and weighed, what is the probability that they will have a mean weight of more than 253 g?

6   The length of a particular species of worm is Normally distributed with mean 5.6 cm and standard deviation 0.4 cm.

(a) What is the probability that a worm chosen at random is longer than 5.7 cm?

(b) Find the probability that the mean length of a sample of 12 worms is greater than 5.7 cm.

B Estimating with confidence (answers p. 122)

Regular checks are made of the water supply to ensure that the degree
of pollution is within acceptable limits. One measure of pollution is
the degree of acidity, or pH value, of the water. Liquids that are
'neutral', that is neither acid nor alkali, have a pH value of 7; a pH
value of less than 7 indicates an acid; a pH greater than 7 indicates an
alkali. EU recommendations specify that safe drinking water should
have a pH of between 6.5 and 8.5.

In Clean Valley, an environmental group claims that the mean pH
is 8.6. Their evidence is based on five random samples of river water.

The members of Class 5 from
Clean Valley Primary School decide
to check the water as part of a
pollution project. They collect
twenty-five jars of water from the
river and calculate a mean pH of 8.5.

The Clean Valley Water Authority,
in an effort to clear its name, selects
a random sample of one hundred
test-tubes of water, and after testing
these calculates that the mean
pH is 8.3.

1D | (a) What justification is there for using the mean pH of a sample
as an estimate for the mean pH of Clean Valley's water supply?

(b) Assuming that the scientific method of each group was of the
same standard, do you think the water of Clean Valley is safe to
drink? Whose evidence would you take most seriously? Discuss
your reasons.

Estimating the mean pH of river water is typical of many statistical
procedures: you cannot measure the whole population, so you use
information from a sample to make estimates of the properties of the
population. For example, you might estimate the population mean by
using the sample mean.

> An **unbiased estimator** is one for which the mean of its
> distribution (i.e. the mean of all possible values of the estimator)
> is equal to the population value it is estimating.
>
> The sample mean is an unbiased estimator of the population mean.

Confidence in how close an estimate is to the actual population mean depends upon the **variability** of the sample mean. For example, suppose you had the evidence of a number of samples, which gave mean values tightly bunched between 7.5 and 8.5, as shown below.

pH levels of 12 water samples

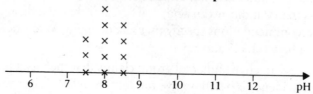

Another batch of samples might produce mean values like this:

pH levels of 12 water samples

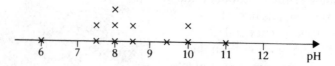

2D   In which of the two cases would you be more confident of predicting the actual pH level of the water? Why?

Confidence is increased when there is less variation in the sample mean values. The first batch clearly has less variability and forms a firmer basis on which to predict the population mean. This suggests that you might use the variance of the sample mean values as a **measure of confidence**.

In Section A you saw that the variance of the distribution of the sample means is equal to the variance of the population divided by the sample size.

$$\text{Variance of } \bar{x} = \frac{\sigma^2}{n}$$

Suppose you know from past experience that the variance of the pH of Clean Valley water is 0.5. Then, for the environmentalists' sample,

$$n = 5, \quad \text{variance of } \bar{x} = \frac{0.5}{5} = 0.1$$

It is standard practice when reporting an estimate such as this to state the size of the sample and its standard deviation. The standard deviation of $\bar{x}$ is called the **standard error** (s.e.).

> The standard deviation of the distribution of the sample means ($\bar{x}$) is called the **standard error** (of the mean).
>
> $$\text{s.e.} = \frac{\sigma}{\sqrt{n}}$$

For the environmentalists' data,

$$\bar{x} = 8.6 \qquad (n = 5, \text{ s.e.} = 0.32)$$

3 Calculate the standard errors of the other two sample means for Clean Valley water. Write them in $\bar{x}$ (n, s.e.) form, as above.

The smaller the standard error of the sample mean, the less variability you can expect in samples, and so the more confidence you can have in your estimate of the population mean.

Exercise B (answers p. 122)

1 Calculate the standard error of the sample mean $\bar{x}$ for a sample of size n from a population of variance σ^2 for these values.

(a) $n = 25, \sigma^2 = 4$ (b) $n = 100, \sigma^2 = 0.9$

2 The following sets of data come from a population whose standard deviation is 2 units. Find $\bar{x}$, n and s.e. for each sample.

(a) 6.0, 7.4, 4.3, 4.6, 5.5, 5.6

(b) 7.3, 6.4, 6.5, 6.8, 5.9, 6.7, 5.0, 8.1, 6.5, 5.0, 6.8, 5.2, 5.9, 8.4, 7.7, 7.1, 7.2, 5.8, 8.9, 7.8

3 Rain falling through clean air is known to have a pH of 5.7 (a little more acidic than most drinking water). Water samples from 40 rainfalls are analysed for pH. The mean pH value of the samples is 3.7. Assuming that the population standard deviation is 0.5, express the result for the sample in $\bar{x}$ (n, s.e.) form. Do you think there is evidence of excess acid in the rain?

C Confidence intervals (answers p. 122)

Stating the size of the sample and the standard error of the mean is one way of expressing how confident you are in your estimate of a population mean, but it is not very 'user-friendly'.

You can express the degree of confidence in your estimate in a more precise way by using an **interval estimate**. The idea is similar that that of tolerance. For example, if a 15 mm panel pin is manufactured to within a tolerance of 1 mm, you could give the length of the pin as

$$15 \text{mm} \pm 1 \text{mm}$$

meaning that all pins have lengths (in millimetres) which lie in the interval (14, 16). If about half the pins have lengths within $\frac{1}{2}$ mm of 15 mm, then you could say that the interval (14.5, 15.5) contains about 50% of the population of pins.

You can use the sample data to construct an interval estimate for the population mean. For example, suppose that in a certain population of adults, height is distributed Normally with a variance of $25\,\text{cm}^2$. The mean height (μ) is unknown. A random sample of 100 adults has mean height 175 cm. What can you say about the mean height of the whole population of adults?

It is clear that a 'point' estimate of the population mean would have to be 175 cm. However, it would be very unlikely that this *was* the mean. It is better to try to estimate a *range* of possible values which you are confident contains the true value.

You know from Section A that the mean of samples ($n = 100$) from $N(\mu, \sigma^2)$ will:

- be Normally distributed
- have mean value μ
- have variance $\dfrac{\sigma^2}{n}$.

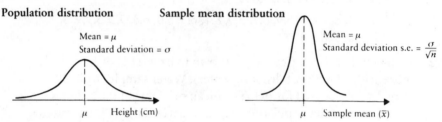

Population distribution   **Sample mean distribution**

Mean = μ Mean = μ
Standard deviation = σ Standard deviation s.e. = $\dfrac{\sigma}{\sqrt{n}}$

μ Height (cm) μ Sample mean ($\bar{x}$)

You know, for example, that 68% of sample mean values are within 1 s.e. of the mean value.

1D | What evidence do you have for this figure?

When you take a sample, you can be 68% **confident** of getting a value for $\bar{x}$ for the sample which lies in the range $\mu \pm 1$ s.e.

You can write this as

$$P(\mu - 1 \text{ s.e.} < \bar{x} < \mu + 1 \text{ s.e.}) = 0.68$$

The inequality can be rearranged to give

$$P(\bar{x} - 1 \text{ s.e.} < \mu < \bar{x} + 1 \text{ s.e.}) = 0.68$$

Since 1 s.e. $= \dfrac{\sigma}{\sqrt{n}} = 0.5$ and $\bar{x} = 175$ cm then you are 68% confident that the interval

$$(175 - 0.5) \text{ to } (175 + 0.5) \qquad \text{i.e. } (174.5, 175.5)$$

contains the true population mean.

The range of values 174.5 to 175.5 is called a 68% **confidence interval for the mean**.

2D If you increase your degree of confidence, what happens to the confidence interval?

3D What proportion of sample means are within 2 standard errors of the true population mean? Calculate another confidence interval which you are much more confident contains the true population mean.

Example 3

The water in a particular lake is known to have pH values with variance 0.5^2.

Environmentalists obtain ten samples of water from the lake and test them. The mean pH of the samples is 8.2.

Obtain an approximate 95% confidence interval for the true population mean pH for the lake.

Solution

Approximately 95% of values of $\bar{x}$ lie within 2 s.e. of the true mean (μ).

So $P(\mu - 2\,\text{s.e.} < \bar{x} < \mu + 2\,\text{s.e.}) = 0.95$

$\Rightarrow P(\bar{x} - 2\,\text{s.e.} < \mu < \bar{x} + 2\,\text{s.e.}) = 0.95$

Now $\bar{x} = 8.2$, $\quad$ s.e. $= \dfrac{\sigma}{\sqrt{n}} = \dfrac{0.5}{\sqrt{10}} = 0.158$, so

$$8.2 - 2 \times 0.158 < \mu < 8.2 + 2 \times 0.158$$
$$7.88 < \mu < 8.52$$

You can be 95% confident that the interval $(7.88, 8.52)$ contains the population mean μ.

4 Children from Clean Valley Primary School collect twenty-five samples of river water. The mean pH of the twenty-five samples is 8.15. The water authority collects one hundred samples with a mean pH of 7.8.

Assume that the variance of pH values for the rive is known to be 0.5. Calculate 68% and 95% confidence intervals for the mean pH from these.

(a) The primary school results

(b) The water authority results

5   Construct a 68% confidence interval and a 95% confidence interval for these.

   (a) A sample with $\bar{x} = 5.57$, $n = 6$, $\sigma = 2$
   (b) A sample with $\bar{x} = 6.75$, $n = 20$, $\sigma = 2$

6   What percentage confidence interval is given by calculating $(\bar{x} - 3\,\text{s.e.}, \bar{x} + 3\,\text{s.e.})$?

Other intervals

For the Normal distribution, 68% and 95% are approximate figures for confidence given by considering **whole** numbers of standard deviations from the sample mean. In practice, confidence intervals are based on 90%, 95% and sometimes 99% confidence. To do this you need to calculate the correct multiple of the standard error that gives these percentages.

7   Use Normal tables to find z, where $\Phi(z) = 0.95$.

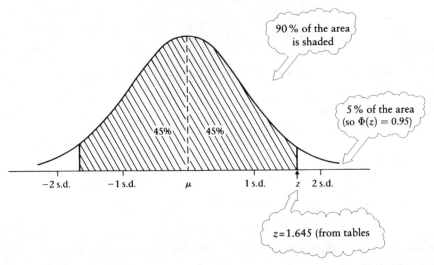

90 % of the area is shaded

5 % of the area (so $\Phi(z) = 0.95$)

45%   45%

−2 s.d.   −1 s.d. μ 1 s.d. z 2 s.d.

$z = 1.645$ (from tables

The 90% confidence interval for μ is $(\bar{x} - 1.645\ \text{s.e.}, \bar{x} + 1.645\ \text{s.e.})$.

8   Show that the **95% confidence interval** for μ is
   $$(\bar{x} - 1.96\,\text{s.e.}, \bar{x} + 1.96\,\text{s.e.}).$$
   Calculate the corresponding 99% confidence interval.

Exercise C (answers p. 123)

1   A sample of size 9 is drawn from a Normal population with standard deviation 10. The sample mean is 20. Calculate 90%, 95% and 99% confidence intervals for the population mean.

2 Suppose the sample in question 1 was of size 25 (rather than 9). Would the calculated confidence intervals be larger or smaller? Calculate them and verify your prediction.

3 Find a 95% confidence interval for a population mean μ, given a population variance σ^2, sample size n and sample mean $\bar{x}$, for these values.

(a) $n = 36$, $\bar{x} = 13.1$, $\sigma^2 = 2.42$

(b) $n = 64$, $\bar{x} = 2.65$, $\sigma^2 = 0.234$

(c) $n = 28$, $\bar{x} = 205$, $\sigma^2 = 83.5$

4 Find a 90% confidence interval for a population mean μ given a population variance of σ^2 and a sample of size n with sample mean $\bar{y}$, for these values.

(a) $n = 125$, $\bar{y} = 0.13$, $\sigma^2 = 0.042$

(b) $n = 60$, $\bar{y} = 20.9$, $\sigma^2 = 3.34$

(c) $n = 55$, $\bar{y} = 845$, $\sigma^2 = 145$

5 A doctor calculates that the mean waiting time for 50 patients is 26 minutes. If the population variance is 6 minutes^2, calculate a 95% confidence interval for the mean waiting time at the surgery.

6 The standard deviation of systolic blood pressure for a population of females is known to be 9.5. The systolic blood pressures of ten women are given below.

>   120   134   128   116   120   132   85   98   125   113

Assuming this is a random sample, construct a 90% confidence interval for the mean systolic blood pressure for this population.

7 A random sample of n measurements is selected from a Normal population with unknown mean μ and standard deviation $\sigma = 10$. Calculate the width of a 95% confidence interval for μ for these values.

(a) $n = 100$ (b) $n = 200$ (c) $n = 400$

Calculate the size of the sample required to give a 95% confidence interval of width 1.

D   Populations with unknown variance (answers p. 123)

Suppose that to each member of the world's population you assign -1 if the person is male and $+1$ if female. Assuming that there are approximately equal numbers of males and females in the world, the distribution of these values has (approximately) $\mu = 0$ and $\sigma^2 = 1$.

1   Check that $\sigma^2 = 1$.

A sample of size 2 from this population
is shown. The sample mean is 0 and
the sample variance is 1.

There are four equally likely combinations:

[male, male], [male, female], [female, male], [female, female]

and so samples of size 2 have the following probability distribution.

Sample	$(-1, -1)$	$(-1, 1)$	$(1, 1)$
Probability	$\frac{1}{4}$	$\frac{1}{2}$	$\frac{1}{4}$
Sample mean, $\bar{x}$	-1	0	1
Sample variance, s^2	0	1	0

2D   (a) Explain the entries in the table above.

(b) Calculate a similar table for samples of size 3.

(c) For both $n = 2$ and $n = 3$, explain how your results illustrate the
fact that $\bar{x}$ is an unbiased estimator of μ.

The distribution of the sample variances is as shown.

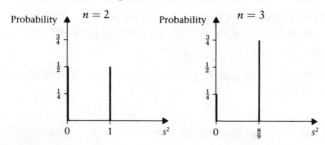

Although the population variance is 1, these distributions have means
of $\frac{1}{2}$ and $\frac{2}{3}$ respectively.

3   When $n = 3$, show that the mean of the distribution of sample
variances is $\frac{2}{3}$.

Unlike the distribution of sample means, the mean of the distribution
of sample variances does *not* equal the population variance. So the
sample variance is not an unbiased estimator of population variance.

The sample variance is a **biased** estimator of the population variance.

It is straightforward (but perhaps tedious) to repeat the calculations of this section for samples of size 4, 5, 6, ... The results, however, are striking.

n	2	3	4	5	6	7	...
Mean of the distribution of s^2	$\frac{1}{2}$	$\frac{2}{3}$	$\frac{3}{4}$	$\frac{4}{5}$	$\frac{5}{6}$	$\frac{6}{7}$	...

As the sample size increases, s^2 looks increasingly good as an estimator for σ^2 (which is equal to 1). However, for small n, it looks as if you should use $\left(\dfrac{n}{n-1}\right)s^2$ as an estimator for σ^2.

Remarkably, this result holds generally, not just for the special distribution considered in this section.

If s^2 is the sample variance of a sample of size n then $\left(\dfrac{n}{n-1}\right)s^2$ is an unbiased estimator of the population variance.

The quantity $\left(\dfrac{n}{n-1}\right)s^2$ is obtained on many calculators by pressing the σ_{n-1} key (instead of σ_n) and then squaring.

A rigorous demonstration that $\left(\dfrac{n}{n-1}\right)s^2$ is an unbiased estimator of σ^2 is beyond the scope of this book. The result is studied further below.

Boxes of matches often have on the side a statement such as:

Average contents 48 matches

Suppose you want to check whether this is true and find out more information about the distribution of the number of matches in a box. The obvious thing to do is to take a random sample of perhaps 1000 matchboxes and count the matches in each. You could then work out the average number of matches in a box and the standard deviation of the number of matches. You could get some idea of the shape of the population distribution by drawing a frequency diagram for your sample of 1000 boxes. This would take a good deal of time and you might find you could only deal practically with a very much smaller number of matchboxes; so it would be useful to see what information can be obtained from much smaller samples.

Taking the problem to its opposite extreme, consider what information could be obtained from a sample of size 2, just two matchboxes, whose contents are counted. Suppose that one box contained 47 matches and the other contained 48 matches. The sample of two boxes has a mean of 47.5 and you can work out the variance as 0.25. To see what can be inferred from this sample you can look at the problem the other way around and assume that you know what the population looks like (its distribution, mean and variance). You can then investigate possible samples of size 2.

Use a simple model for the population: assume that 20% of boxes contain 47 matches, 60% contain 48 matches and 20% contain 49 matches.

x	47	48	49
$P(X=x)$	0.2	0.6	0.2

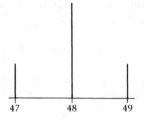

4E Show that the population mean is 48 and that the population variance is 0.4.

If a random sample of two boxes is chosen from the population, then there are just 9 possibilities.

> A sample of 48, 49 has probability 0.12

Probabilities

	47	48	49
47	0.04	0.12	0.04
48	0.12	0.36	0.12
49	0.04	0.12	0.04

Values of $\bar{x}$

	47	48	49
47	47.0	47.5	48.0
48	47.5	48.0	48.5
49	48.0	48.5	49.0

Values of s^2

	47	48	49
47	0.00	0.25	1.00
48	0.25	0.00	0.25
49	1.00	0.25	0.00

5E Show that the probability of obtaining a sample having $\bar{x} = 48.5$ is 0.24.

$\bar{x}$ and s^2 have these distributions:

Sample mean $\bar{x}$

x	47.0	47.5	48.0	48.5	49.0
$P(\bar{x} = x)$	0.04	0.24	0.44	0.24	0.04

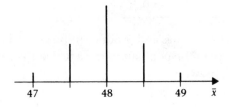

Sample variance s^2

y	0	0.25	1
$P(s^2 = y)$	0.44	0.48	0.08

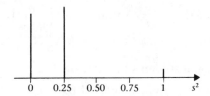

The original distribution was symmetrical. Note that $\bar{x}$ has a symmetrical distribution, but that s^2 does not.

6E (a) Show that the mean value of the distribution of $\bar{x}$ is 48.

(b) Show that the mean value of the distribution of s^2 is 0.2.

Comparing these values with $\mu = 48$ and $\sigma^2 = 0.4$, you can see that if you took a large number of samples of size 2, the distribution of their means ($\bar{x}$) would be symmetrical and have mean value μ; but the distribution of their variance (s^2) would have a mean value of only $\frac{1}{2}\sigma^2$.

7E   Investigate, taking samples of size 2 from the other populations of matches (below).

	Rectangular		
x	47	48	49
$P(X = x)$	$\frac{1}{3}$	$\frac{1}{3}$	$\frac{1}{3}$

	Asymmetrical		
x	47	48	49
$P(X = x)$	0.6	0.3	0.1

	U-shaped		
x	47	48	49
$P(X = x)$	0.5	0	0.5

Comment on your findings and produce unbiased estimates for the mean and variance of the population from which the original sample of two boxes was drawn.

You could use a computer simulation to investigate samples of size other than 2.

Exercise D (answers p. 124)

1   Use the relevant formulas and the statistical functions on your calculator to calculate the sample variance and $\left(\dfrac{n}{n-1}\right)s^2$ for each of the following samples.

(a)   The heights of eight students in metres:

1.54,   1.66,   1.62,   1.68,   1.65,   1.63,   1.67,   1.65

(b)   The speeds of ten cars entering a village in km h^{-1}:

45,   40,   49,   53,   48,   57,   50,   60,   47,   56

2   Calculate s^2 for each of the following samples. Hence write down an estimate of the population variance.

(a)   The sizes of men's shoes sold in one week in a shoe shop:

Size	39	40	41	42	43	44	45	46
Pairs sold	1	6	13	20	25	14	7	1

(b)   The lifetimes in minutes of twenty batteries:

Lifetime (min)	0–60	60–90	90–120	120–150	150–180	180–210	210–240
Number of batteries	1	0	1	5	7	4	2

3 An inspector of weights and measures selects at random six bags of flour from a consignment and finds the weights in kilograms to be 1.502, 1.499, 1.506, 1.497, 1.501, 1.503. Find unbiased estimates for the mean and variance of the weights of the bags in this entire consignment of flour.

E Using estimated variances (answers p. 125)

So far, to calculate confidence intervals, you have assumed:

- that you know the standard deviation of the population (so that you can work out the standard error of the sample mean)
- that the distribution of the sample mean is Normal.

1D | Are these reasonable assumptions? What can you do if they are not?

Suppose you conduct clinical trials for a drug company and are testing a drug to see how effective it is. For 29 patients with the same disease, you measure the remission time (the number of days' relief from symptoms after taking the drug). These remission times in days are as follows:

5, 12, 7, 24, 1, 23, 20, 23, 15, 20, 5, 13, 15, 16, 9,
2, 13, 34, 21, 19, 12, 2, 13, 12, 10, 3, 4, 6, 35

2D | (a) From these data, can you calculate the standard error of the mean remission time?

(b) Do you know the population standard deviation in this case? What could you use instead?

(c) Do you think the distribution of remission time is likely to be Normal? Is the distribution of *mean* remission time Normal?

The population variance is often not known when calculating confidence intervals from samples. In this case you can use the sample standard deviation to estimate the population standard deviation.

You will recall that there are *two* possible estimators for the population variance: the sample variance itself, s^2, and $\dfrac{ns^2}{(n-1)}$.

There is a variety of notations for these values. It is conventional to denote them by s_n^2 and s_{n-1}^2, respectively.

> s_n^2 is the variance of the sample of n data values.
>
> $s_{n-1}^2 = \dfrac{n}{n-1} s_n^2$ is an unbiased estimator for σ^2.

s_n^2 is biased, whereas s_{n-1}^2 is unbiased. However, when n is large, the difference between these two estimators becomes insignificant and for large samples (for example $n > 25$) you can use the variance of the sample as your estimate of the population variance.

3 For the remission data above, calculate 95% confidence limits for the population mean, using each of these as an estimator for the population variance.

(a) s_n^2 (b) s_{n-1}^2

Throughout this chapter, s_{n-1}^2 is used to estimate the population variance, on the grounds that it is unbiased.

Example 4

A random sample of 15 visitors to the York Viking Museum showed that they had waited the following times (in minutes) to get in.

$$19, 28, 34, 10, 27, 31, 25, 37, 54, 27, 54, 8, 17, 24, 21$$

Estimate a 95% confidence interval for the mean waiting time.

Solution

Working in minutes, the sample has mean 27.73.
The variance of the sample values is 165.3.

An unbiased estimate of the population variance (s_{n-1}^2) is

$$\frac{15}{14} \times 165.3 = 177.1.$$

An estimate of the standard error is $\dfrac{\sqrt{177.1}}{\sqrt{15}} = 3.44$.

The 95% confidence interval for waiting time is 27.73 ± 1.96 s.e. minutes, i.e. $(21.0, 34.5)$ minutes.

Note that when the background population is *not* Normal, the distribution of the sample mean becomes more and more nearly Normal for larger and larger samples. You have met this idea before as the **Central Limit Theorem**.

Exercise E (answers p. 125)

1 Calculate an approximate 95% confidence interval for the population mean using the following sample data.

(a) $n = 36$, $\bar{x} = 10$, sample variance $= 4$

(b) $n = 100$, $\bar{x} = 20$, sample variance $= 9$

(c) $n = 5$, $\bar{x} = 20$, $s_n^2 = 0.01$

Give a reason why your answer to part (c) may be unreliable.

2 In an alpine skiing competition, the times taken by 59 competitors to complete the course gave a mean of 1 minute 54 seconds. The standard deviation of the sample was 4.1 seconds. Calculate a 90% confidence interval for the mean time to complete the course.

3 A population of small fish was sampled, giving the following age distribution.

Age (years)	1	2	3	4	5	6	7	8	9
Frequency	0	80	345	243	124	56	34	6	3

Find an approximate 95% confidence interval for the mean age of this population of fish. Write down in your own words how you would explain the meaning of this interval to a local fisherman who has not been taught statistics.

4 (a) Calculate a 90% confidence interval for the population mean based on a sample with $n = 10$, $\bar{x} = 10$ and $s_n = 4$.

(b) Why is the interval not reliable in this case?

F Population proportions (answers p. 126)

Suppose that a biologist wants to find out how many fish there are in a lake.

One commonly-used method is the 'capture–recapture' technique. The biologist catches a number of the fish, for example 50, marks them in some way, and puts them back into the lake. Some time later she catches a batch of 40 fish and observes how many of them are marked.

1D   If 5 of the 40 fish caught are marked, what should be her estimate of the total number of fish in the lake?

How accurate do you think this estimate will be?

This experiment simulates the capture–recapture method for a population of unknown size. Your task is to estimate the number of tiles in a bag using capture–recapture.

You need a bag of white tiles (an unknown number but somewhere in the region of 200–300). Replace 50 of the white tiles with coloured tiles.

Select a sample of 25 tiles from the bag and count how many of them are coloured.

What proportion of your sample is coloured?

What is your estimate of the number of tiles in the bag?

Repeat the experiment about 20 times (keeping the same number of tiles in the bag). Record each estimate. Empty the bag and count the total number of tiles that it contains.

Calculate the average of your estimates.

2   How good a method do you think this is?

Give a reason for your answer.

Opinion polls

One important area of application of some of the ideas encountered in this unit is that of trying to find out how the population would vote in an election. Newspapers and television companies often engage professional organisations (such as Mori or Gallup) to conduct an opinion poll for them. The poll is of a carefully selected random sample of the population. Your earlier work has been about obtaining information on a population mean from a sample. Most opinion polls set out to tackle another problem – what **proportion** (or percentage) of the population will vote for a particular party.

For example, suppose that a survey of 400 randomly selected adults shows that 144 will vote Conservative at the next general election. To obtain a 95% confidence limit for the proportion of the population which will vote Conservative, you can proceed as follows:

Let p be the proportion of the population who will vote Conservative. Although p is not known, an estimate would be $\frac{144}{400} = 0.36$. You need a confidence interval for this estimate.

Let X be the number of people in a sample who will vote Conservative. Then $X \sim B(400, p)$.

3 Explain why X has this distribution.

$$\text{Mean } (X) = np = 400p$$
$$\text{Variance } (X) = np(1 - p) = 400p(1 - p)$$

For large samples ($n = 400$ here) you can approximate this distribution with a Normal distribution having the same mean and variance. So:

$$X \sim N(400p, 400p(1-p))$$

For 95% of samples,

$$400p - 1.96\sqrt{400p(1-p)} < X < 400p + 1.96\sqrt{400p(1-p)} \quad (1)$$

$$\Rightarrow \frac{X}{400} - 1.96\sqrt{\frac{p(1-p)}{400}} < p < \frac{X}{400} + 1.96\sqrt{\frac{p(1-p)}{400}} \quad (2)$$

4 Carefully show how inequality 2 can be deduced from inequality 1.

The interval you have obtained is the 95% confidence interval for p, the proportion of the population which will vote Conservative. Unfortunately, the expression cannot be evaluated as you cannot work out $\sqrt{\dfrac{p(1-p)}{400}}$ because p is not known! Since you have a large sample, however, you can take the sample value $\dfrac{x}{400} = 0.36$ as an estimate of p. So, approximately,

$$0.36 - 1.96\sqrt{\frac{0.36 \times 0.64}{400}} < p < 0.36 + 1.96\sqrt{\frac{0.36 \times 0.64}{400}}$$

You can be 95% confident that between 31.3% and 40.7% of the population will vote Conservative. In general:

> If p_s is the proportion in a sample of size n, the 95% confidence interval for the population is
>
> $$p_s - 1.96\sqrt{\frac{p_s(1-p_s)}{n}} < p < p_s + 1.96\sqrt{\frac{p_s(1-p_s)}{n}}$$

Example 5

A school of 300 pupils has 42 who are left-handed. Obtain a 95% confidence interval for the proportion of the population (p) who are left-handed.

Solution

The proportion of left-handed pupils in the school $= \dfrac{42}{300} = 0.14$.

A 95% confidence interval for the population proportion (p) is

$$0.14 - 1.96\sqrt{\frac{0.14 \times 0.86}{300}} < p < 0.14 + 1.96\sqrt{\frac{0.14 \times 0.86}{300}}$$

$0.10 < p < 0.18$ (to 2 s.f.) i.e. between 10% and 18%.

Exercise F (answers p. 126)

LATEST GALLUP SNAPSHOT

If there were a General Election tomorrow, which party would you support?

	Early Mar	**Now**	Change
Labour	57$^1/_2$	**55$^1/_2$**	−2
Conservative	23	**26**	+3
Lib Democrats	16	**15$^1/_2$**	−$^1/_2$
Other	3$^1/_2$	**3**	−$^1/_2$
Lab lead	34$^1/_2$	**29$^1/_2$**	−5

The figures are based on a sample of 1,119 electors interviewed between Mar 27 and April 1 in 100 districts across Great Britain.

MARCH GALLUP 9000

If there were a General Election tomorrow, which party would you support?

	1992 Election	Jan	Feb	**Mar**	Change
Lab	35·2	55·6	55·4	**57·3**	+1·9
Con	42·8	23·1	25·4	**23·9**	−1·5
L Dem	18·3	16·8	14·9	**15·1**	+0·2
Other	3·7	4·4	4·4	**3·7**	−0·7
Lab lead	−7·6	32·5	30·0	**33·4**	+3·4

The figures are based on 10,284 interviews conducted face-to-face between Feb 29 and April 2 in more than 350 districts across Great Britain.

THE GOVERNMENT

Do you approve or disapprove of the Government's record to date?

	1992 Election	Feb	**Mar**	Change
Approve	29·4	14·4	**13·3**	−1·1
Disapp	57·0	74·7	**75·3**	+0·6

THE LEADERS

Who would make the best Prime Minister, Mr Major, Mr Blair or Mr Ashdown?

	1992 Election	Feb	**Mar**	Change
*Blair	27·7	38·2	**41·8**	+3·6
Major	39·1	18·3	**17·8**	−0·5
Ashdown	17·1	14·9	**13·9**	−1·0

*1992 election figure refers to Mr Kinnock

THE FEEL GOOD FACTOR

How do you think the financial situation of your household will change over the next 12 months?

	1992 Election	Jan	Feb	**Mar**	Change
Get a lot/ a little better	28·9	20·5	19·7	**19·5**	−0·2
Get a little/ a lot worse	16·3	26·3	28·7	**29·4**	+0·7
Difference	+12·6	−5·8	−9·0	**−9·9**	−0·9

ECONOMIC COMPETENCE

With Britain in economic difficulties, which party do you think could handle the problem best – the Conservatives or Labour?

	1992 Election	Jan	Feb	**Mar**	Change
Labour	38·0	45·4	44·6	**46·9**	+2·3
Conservative	44·6	22·8	24·1	**22·8**	−1·3
Lab advantage	−6·6	22·6	20·5	**24·1**	+3·6

The Gallup 9000 survey is large enough for its findings to be reported to one decimal place. In the case of the smaller snapshot survey, the findings are reported to the nearest whole or half number.
Those who refused to answer any questions or replied 'don't know' have been excluded from the above percentages. In the March Gallup 9000 the total was 15·5 per cent; in the latest snapshot survey it was 14$\frac{1}{2}$ per cent.

1 The extract is from an article in the *Daily Telegraph* of 5 April 1996. Read the article and answer the questions.
The Gallup sample was based on 10 284 interviews.

(a) Calculate 95% confidence intervals for the proportion of the population in March 1996 who thought that each of these was the best person to be Prime Minister.

   (i) Mr Major   (ii) Mr Blair

(b) In the main part of the report (the second table), 57.3% of the population said they would vote Labour. Calculate a 90% confidence interval for the population proportion.

(c) The 'snapshot' figures (the first table) are based on a sample of only 1119 people. $55\frac{1}{2}\%$ said they would vote Labour. Find a 99% confidence interval for the population proportion who will vote Labour.

(d) The author states that for the Gallup 9000 poll it is acceptable to report the percentages correct to 1 decimal place. Confirm that this is so.

2   This old newspaper cutting shows the results of a poll of 750 travellers on British Rail following a bomb scare at a London main-line station.

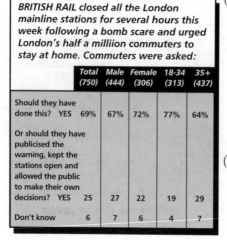

BRITISH RAIL closed all the London mainline stations for several hours this week following a bomb scare and urged London's half a milliion commuters to stay at home. Commuters were asked:

	Total (750)	Male (444)	Female (306)	18-34 (313)	35+ (437)
Should they have done this? YES	69%	67%	72%	77%	64%
Or should they have publicised the warning, kept the stations open and allowed the public to make their own decisions? YES	25	27	22	19	29
Don't know	6	7	6	4	7

Evening Standard

(a) (i) Calculate 95% confidence limits for the proportion of male travellers who felt British Rail were correct in advising passengers to stay at home.

   (ii) Do the same for female travellers.

(b) Calculate a 90% confidence interval for the proportion of 18–34-year-olds who felt British Rail should have let passengers make up their own minds.

3   A biologist marks 50 fish in a lake. Two days later she returns and catches 30 fish, 12 of which are marked.

(a) Calculate a 95% confidence interval for the proportion of marked fish in the lake.

(b) Hence work out a 95% confidence estimate for the number of fish in the lake.

4   A local council conducts a quick poll and discovers that about 50% of people would support a new shopping complex. In order to estimate this proportion more accurately (to within ±2%) it decides to have a second poll of size n. Calculate n for these.

(a) 90% confidence   (b) 95% confidence

After working through this chapter you should

1 understand that the mean of a sample will have its own distribution, **the sampling distribution of the mean**

2 know the Central Limit Theorem, which states that, when sampling from a population:
   - the distribution of the sample means is approximately Normal if the sample size is large enough
   - the mean of the distribution of the sample means is equal to the population mean
   - the variance of the distribution of the sample means is the variance of the parent population divided by the sample size

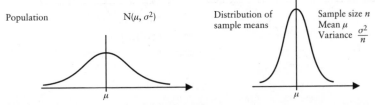

3 appreciate that any statistic taken from a sample will have its own distribution and may be used to estimate measures for the whole population

4 know what the terms **biased** and **unbiased estimators** mean

5 know that the sample mean is an unbiased estimator of the population mean

6 know that, for a sample size n, the sample variance s^2 is a biased estimator of the population variance but $\dfrac{ns^2}{n-1}$ is unbiased

7 understand that the standard error of the sample mean gives a measure of how close the sample mean is likely to be to the population mean

8 understand the idea of a **confidence interval** for the population mean, and be able to construct 90%, 95% and 99% confidence intervals from a sample of population with known variance

9 know how to construct confidence intervals for the mean of a population when the variance is not necessarily known, using a large sample

10 be able to calculate approximate confidence intervals for a population proportion based on a large sample

11 know that if the proportion in a sample of size n is p_s then a 95% confidence interval for the population proportion is

$$\left(p_s - 1.96\sqrt{\frac{p_s(1-p_s)}{n}}, \quad p_s + 1.96\sqrt{\frac{p_s(1-p_s)}{n}} \right)$$

7 Expectation and variance

A Expected value E(x) (answers p. 127)

1D
- If you roll a six-sided die (numbered 1–6) what would you *expect* the score to be?
- What makes this question difficult to answer?
- If you were to roll the die a large number of times what do you think the *average* score would be close to?

2 Imagine rolling a fair six-sided die 100 times.

(a) Copy and complete the following table.

Score (s)	$P(S = s)$	'Expected' frequency in 100 rolls, f	fs
1			
2			
3			
4			
5			
6			

(b) Find the expected average by calculating $\dfrac{\Sigma fs}{\Sigma f}$.

(c) Repeat the above table for rolling the die 6000 times and again calculate the expected average.

(d) Copy and complete the following table for the same die.

Score (s)	$P(S = s)$	$s \times P(S = s)$
1		
2		
3		
4		
5		
6		

(e) Find $\Sigma s\, P(S = s)$.

(f) What do you notice about your answers to parts (b), (c) and (e)? What do you think the 'expected average' would be if the die was rolled 20 000 times?

> When an experiment yielding a discrete random variable x is repeated a large number of terms, the 'expected average' (called the **expectation**) of x is given by
>
> $$E(x) = \sum_{\text{all } x} x\,P(x).$$

3 Write out a probability distribution for T, the total score when two dice are rolled together, and use it to find the expected value, $E(T)$.

Exercise A (answers p. 127)

1 Y is the discrete random variable with the following probability distribution.

y	$P(Y = y)$
1	0.5
2	0.25
3	0.25

Find $E(Y)$.

2 A game is played in which the score S is determined by rolling a fair six-sided die and tossing a fair coin. If the coin shows heads then the score on the die is doubled to give S, but if tails, then the final score S is as shown on the die. Find $E(S)$.

3 A card is drawn randomly from a standard pack of 52 and given its face value V with Jack, Queen and King all counting for a value of 10. Find $E(V)$.

4 The discrete random variable X has the following probability distribution.

x	0	1	2	3	4
$P(X = x)$	0.6	0.1	0.2	0.07	p

Find p and hence find $E(X)$.

B Expectation of a function of a random variable (answers p. 128)

1 Suppose a new discrete random variable $P(=2S)$ is obtained by doubling the score, S, shown on an ordinary die when it is rolled.

Then we can find $E(P)$ by writing out a probability distribution for p.

s	$p = 2s$	$P(P = p)$

Copy and complete the table and use it to find $E(P)$.

2 Now consider the discrete random variable R where $R = P + 3$ (that is R is obtained by rolling a die, doubling the score and then adding 3). Make a similar probability distribution table for R and use it to find $E(R)$.

3 Write R in terms of S.
Write $E(R)$ in terms of $E(S)$.

4 If random variable X is such that $E(X) = \mu$ suggest values for these, where a and b are constants.

   (a) $E(aX)$

   (b) $E(X + b)$

   (c) $E(aX + b)$

5E Consider the random variable S^2 obtained by squaring the score S in question 1.

s	s^2	$P(S^2 = s^2)$	$s^2 \times P(S^2 = s^2)$
1	1		
2	4		
3	9		
4	16		
5	25		
6	36		

   (a) Copy and complete the table above and hence find
   $$E(S^2) = \Sigma s^2 P(S^2 = s^2)$$

   (b) In a similar way find these.

      (i) $E(S^2 + 2)$

      (ii) $E(S^2 + S)$

      (iii) $E(S^3)$

The expectation of a discrete random variable X is
$$E(X) = \sum x \, P(X = x)$$
The expectation of a function $g(X)$ of a discrete random variable X is
$$E(g(X)) = \sum g(x)P(X = x)$$
A particularly important example is
$$E(X^2) = \sum x^2 P(X = x)$$
Note also that if X and Y are independent random variables and a, b, c are constants then
$$E(aX + bY + c) = aE(X) + bE(Y) + c.$$

Theoretical variance $V(X)$

6 Consider question 2(a) on page 96. Extend the table by adding an fs^2 column and use this to calculate the 'expected variance' of the die using $\dfrac{\sum fs^2}{\sum f} - \bar{s}^2$.

7 Now, by extending the table in question 2(d) on page 96 with a column $s^2 \times P(S = s)$, calculate a theoretical variance for S using the formula
$$V(S) = E(S^2) - (E(S))^2.$$
Comment on your answer with respect to question 6 above.

8 X is the discrete random variable obtained from a binomial distribution $X \sim B(5, 0.5)$. By making a table find $E(X)$ and $V(X)$.

9D Using the definition of $V(X)$
show that $\qquad V(aX) = a^2 V(X)$
and $\qquad V(aX + b) = a^2 V(X).$

These results summarise what you have found.

$$V(X) = E(X^2) - (E(X))^2$$
$$\text{which is often written as } E(X^2) - E^2(X)$$
$$V(aX) = a^2 V(X)$$
$$V(aX + b) = a^2 V(X)$$

Here are some further results.

$$E(X + Y) = E(X) + E(Y)$$
$$E(X - Y) = E(X) - E(Y)$$

$$V(X + Y) = V(X) + V(Y)$$
$$V(X - Y) = V(X) + V(Y)$$

$$E(aX + bY + c) = aE(X) + bE(Y) + c$$
$$V(aX + bY + c) = a^2V(X) + b^2V(Y)$$

10D   Plan and carry out some practical activities to verify these results.

The mean and variance of B(*n, p*) – a proof

The results of the previous sections can be used to prove results for the mean and variance of a binomial random variable. A binomial variable occurs when you are considering the total number of times a given event occurs in n independent trials. For example, the trial might be the throwing of a coin and the outcome might be the occurrence of a head. The total number of heads occurring when, for example, four coins are thrown would be a binomial random variable taking values of 0, 1, 2, 3 or 4.

Suppose the outcome of a particular trial occurs with probability p and does not occur with probability $(1 - p)$ or q.

There are 0 or 1 occurrences in a given trial.

Let X be the number of occurrences in a trial. X takes values in $\{0, 1\}$. The probability distribution for X is

x	0	1
$P(X = x)$	q	p

11   Show that the mean and variance of X are p and pq respectively.

Now, for n trials, define the binomial variable R, where
$$R = X_1 + X_2 + \ldots + X_n \quad \text{and} \quad R \sim B(n, p)$$
$$\Rightarrow E[R] = E[X_1 + X_2 + \ldots + X_n]$$
$$= E[X_1] + E[X_2] + \ldots + E[X_n] \qquad (1)$$
$$= E[X] + E[X] + \ldots + E[X] \qquad (2)$$
$$= n \times E[X]$$
$$= np$$

12 In the argument given above, explain why lines 1 and 2 are correct.

Also, for the variance $V[R]$,

$$V[R] = V[X_1 + X_2 + \ldots + X_n]$$
$$= V[X_1] + V[X_2] + \ldots + V[X_n]$$
$$= V[X] + V[X] + \ldots + V[X]$$
$$= nV[X]$$
$$= npq$$

If $R \sim B(n, p)$ then

$$E[R] = np$$

$$V[R] = npq$$

Exercise B (answers p. 129)

1 (a) For $Y \sim B(6, \frac{1}{3})$ find $E(Y)$ and $V(Y)$.

(b) Using your answers to part (a) find $E(2Y)$ and $V(2Y)$.

2 In a game it is possible to score 0, 1, 2 or 3. A particular player scores 0 with probability 0.5, 1 with probability 0.2, 2 with probability 0.2.

S is the random variable representing her score.

(a) Find $P(S = 3)$.

(b) Find $E(S)$ and $V(S)$.

(c) After reaching a certain point in the game, the players' scores are trebled on any given turn.

Find $E(3S)$ and $V(3S)$.

3 T is the sum of the scores on rolling two dice.

Find $E(T)$ and $V(T)$.

Why is this *not* the same as the result of doubling the score on one die roll?

After working through this chapter you should

1 be able to calculate $E(X)$ and $V(X)$ for a discrete random variable

2 be able to calculate $E(Y)$ and $V(Y)$ where Y is a simple function of X

3 know that random variables may be combined to give composite variables

4 understand the term **expectation** as applied to random variables and be familiar with the notation of expectation

5 know that for **independent** random variables:

   (a) $E(X \pm Y) = E(X) \pm E(Y)$
   (b) $V(X \pm Y) = V(X) + V(Y)$

6 be able to obtain the formulas for the mean and variance of a binomial random variable.

Answers

1 The binomial distribution

A Probability and Pascal's triangle
(p. 1)

1D There are more paths leading to a central slot than to an outside one. Assuming that each path is equally likely to be taken by a ball, more balls will end up in the central slots than in the outside ones.

2 There are three routes; each one is equally likely and each has probability $\frac{1}{8}$. Therefore P(slot 2) $= \frac{3}{8}$.

3

x	0	1	2	3
$P(X=x)$	$\frac{1}{8}$	$\frac{3}{8}$	$\frac{3}{8}$	$\frac{1}{8}$

4 For 400 balls you would expect $400 \times \frac{1}{8} = 50$ in slot 0, and so on:

Slot X	0	1	2	3
Expected number	50	150	150	50

5

x	0	1	2
$P(X=x)$	$\frac{1}{4}$	$\frac{1}{2}$	$\frac{1}{4}$

Expected frequencies are 100, 200, 100.

6 The ball will hit 4 pins. The probability of a particular route is $(\frac{1}{2})^4 = \frac{1}{16}$.

7 Routes to P $= 1$. Routes to Q $= 3$.

There are therefore $1 + 3 = 4$ routes to slot 1. P(slot 1) $= \frac{4}{16} = \frac{1}{4}$.

8

Slot X	0	1	2	3	4
Routes	1	4	6	4	1

x	0	1	2	3	4
$P(x)$	$\frac{1}{16}$	$\frac{4}{16}$	$\frac{6}{16}$	$\frac{4}{16}$	$\frac{1}{16}$

9D Calculators use different methods but many use, for example, 7C2 for $\binom{7}{2}$. Some sets of mathematical tables show these values.

Exercise A (p. 4)

1 (a) 35   (b) 21   (c) 15   (d) 10
(e) 2   (f) 35   (g) 5   (h) 1

2 (a) 21   (b) 21

If exactly 2 heads are obtained in 7 throws then exactly 5 tails must also occur. This tells you that $\binom{7}{2}$ and $\binom{7}{5}$ must be equal.

3 $\frac{28}{256}$

4 $\frac{5}{16}$

5 (a) $\frac{1}{32}$ (b) $\frac{5}{16}$

6 $\frac{252}{1024} = 0.246$ (to 3 s.f.)

B The binomial probability model
(p. 5)

1 (a) The ball is deflected R L R. The probability that the ball will take the route shown is $0.4 \times 0.6 \times 0.4 = 0.096$.

Assume that each deflection (L or R) is independent of previous ones.

(b) Other routes are R R L and L R R. The probabilities are both $0.4^2 \times 0.6 = 0.096$.

(c) There are 3 equally likely ways to arrive in slot 2.

P(slot 2) $= 3 \times 0.096 = 0.288$

(d) P(slot 0) $= 1 \times (0.6)^3 = 0.216$
    Route: L L L
P(slot 1) $= 3 \times (0.6)^2(0.4) = 0.432$
    Routes: L L R, L R L, R L L
P(slot 3) $= 1 \times (0.4)^3 = 0.064$
    Route: R R R

(e) The expected frequencies are

Slot	0	1	2	3
Number of balls	108	216	144	32

(f)

x	$P(x)$	
0	$1 \times (0.6)^5$	$= 0.07776$
1	$5 \times (0.4) \times (0.6)^4$	$= 0.2592$
2	$10 \times (0.4)^2 \times (0.6)^3$	$= 0.3456$
3	$10 \times (0.4)^3 \times (0.6)^2$	$= 0.2304$
4	$5 \times (0.4)^4 \times (0.6)$	$= 0.0768$
5	$1 \times (0.4)^5$	$= 0.01024$

(g)

x	$P(x)$	
0	$1 \times (0.2)^3$	$= 0.008$
1	$3 \times (0.8) \times (0.2)^2$	$= 0.096$
2	$3 \times (0.8)^2 \times (0.2)$	$= 0.384$
3	$1 \times (0.8)^3$	$= 0.512$

2D (a) As the subsequent explanation shows, this does not prove Murphy's law.

(b) This would be much more convincing support for Murphy's law.

Exercise B (p. 9)

1 $S =$ the number of sixes when 4 dice are thrown

The probability of no sixes

$$= \frac{5}{6} \times \frac{5}{6} \times \frac{5}{6} \times \frac{5}{6}$$

The probability of 1 six

$$= \binom{4}{1} \times \frac{1}{6} \times \left(\frac{5}{6}\right)^3$$

The probability of 2 sixes

$$= \binom{4}{2} \times \left(\frac{1}{6}\right)^2 \times \left(\frac{5}{6}\right)^2$$

The probability of 3 sixes

$$= \binom{4}{3} \times \left(\frac{1}{6}\right)^3 \times \frac{5}{6}$$

The probability of 4 sixes

$$= \binom{4}{4} \times \left(\frac{1}{6}\right)^4$$

s	0	1	2	3	4
$P(S=s)$	0.482	0.386	0.116	0.015	0.001

2 (a) If Wizzo is no better or worse than Wow then the probability that 1 person prefers Wizzo is $\frac{1}{2}$.

The probability that exactly 8 prefer

Wizzo is $\binom{10}{8} \times \left(\frac{1}{2}\right)^{10} = 0.044$

The probability that 9 prefer Wizzo is

$$\binom{10}{9} \times \left(\frac{1}{2}\right)^{10} = 0.010$$

The probability that all 10 prefer

Wizzo is $1 \times \left(\frac{1}{2}\right)^{10} = 0.001$

So the probability of 8 or more is
$0.044 + 0.010 + 0.001 = 0.055$

(b) P(8 or more prefer Wizzo) $= 0.678$
(to 3 s.f.)

3 0.298

4 0.284 (to 3 s.f.)

Since what happens in one year could influence the next (there may be the same crews for example) the assumption of independence is very weak. It is likely that the probability of Cambridge's success is *not* the same each year.

5 (a) 0.0355 (to 3 s.f.)

(b) 0.000 17 (to 2 s.f.)

This is a very unlikely event, so you should doubt the player's honesty!

6 P(9 *or more* wins) $= 0.0107$ (to 3 s.f.)
The captain is therefore extremely lucky.

7 The probability of rain on 6 or more days out is 7 is

$$\binom{7}{6} \times \left(\frac{1}{3}\right)^2 \times \left(\frac{2}{3}\right) + \left(\frac{1}{3}\right)^7$$
$$= 0.0069 \text{ (to 2 s.f.)}$$

The Wilsons were very unlucky with the weather. The model is almost certainly not appropriate – the assumption of independence is weak.

8 If both drinks were the same you would expect the probability that 7 or more out of 8 would prefer the new flavour to be

$$\binom{8}{7} \times \left(\frac{1}{2}\right)^8 + \left(\frac{1}{2}\right)^8 = 0.0352 \text{ (to 3 s.f.)}$$

This result is clearly unlikely and suggests that the new flavour is preferred.

9   (a)   The probability that at least one seed will germinate out of the five planted is the same as

1 – probability that *no* seeds germinate
$$= 1 - (0.8)^5$$
$$= 0.672\,32$$

(b) $1 - (0.8)^n = 0.9$
$$0.1 = (0.8)^n$$

This can be solved by 'trial and improvement' on a calculator, or you can take natural logarithms of both sides.

$$\ln(0.1) = n \ln(0.8)$$
$$n = \frac{\ln(0.1)}{\ln(0.8)}$$
$$n = 10.3$$

Thus 11 or more seeds must be planted to ensure a 90% chance of at least one germination.

C   Sampling (p. 10)

1D   There are several reasons why you might wish to sample a parent population rather than test every member of the population.

- There would be little point in a car manufacturer collision-testing every car produced. There would be no cars left to sell! Some items need to be 'tested to destruction' to see how strong or safe they are. Motorcycle helmets, climbers' ropes and steel for building bridges are some examples.

- If you wanted people's opinions about something, for example which party they would vote for if there were a general election tomorrow, it would be very costly and time-consuming to interview every voter in the country.

- Wine tasters sample just a small mouthful of wine to judge its quality. Sampling from a large vat of wine enables the quality of hundreds of bottles to be ascertained.

A 'good' sample should:
- be representative of the parent population
- enable you to find out what you want to know about the parent population.

2D   (a)   It is quite likely that neither sampling procedure gives particularly close estimates to the true mean (μ). Neither sampling method is likely to give a representative sample, due in part to the way in which the data are listed on the sheet. Method A will always give a sample of five students of the same sex, while method B will sometimes give a mixed group. Neither will give a sample of five independently selected individuals. If a particular sixth-former is selected, then the other members of the sample are adjacent or close by on the list.

(b)   To obtain a more representative sample, you must ensure that each member of the population has an equal and independent chance of being included. This type of sample is called a **random sample**. An elementary but time-consuming way of obtaining such a sample would be to number the sixth-formers from 1 to 300 and then to draw five numbers from 300 well-mixed raffle tickets.

A computer or calculator can be used to rapidly generate random numbers in the range 1 to 300. Some calculators generate random integers in the range 0 to 9, so three such numbers taken together give a number in the range 000 to 999, each with an equal probability of occurring. If each sixth-former is allocated one number you would not be able to make a selection if any of random numbers 301–999 appeared. To avoid this wastage you can allocate three numbers to each person.

	Numbers allocated		
Student 1	001	301	601
Student 2	002	302	602
......	...	...	...
......	...	...	...
Student 300	300	600	900

In this scheme only the numbers 000 and 901–999 remain unused. However, it is not possible to allocate these numbers, as each sixth former must have an equal number of 'chances' so that each has an equal probability of $\frac{1}{300}$ of being included in the sample.

3 (a) The sample is biased.

Possible reasons are:

(i)   One elderly person with a contagious disease is more likely to pass it on to another elderly person in the residential home than if he or she were living alone.

(ii) People in a residential home are more likely to be in need of medical attention.

(iii) Elderly people living in a residential home are likely to have better living conditions (food, heating etc.) than those not living in a residential home.

(iv) If the home is fee-paying then residents are unlikely to be representative of the general population.

(b) The sample was biased.

In fact Truman won the 1984 US Presidential Election. The incorrect forecast of the opinion poll was attributed to the fact that the majority of telephone owners in the US in 1948 were Republican voters. Those who owned telephones did not form a representative sample of the voting population.

(c) The sample is biased.

In November the main reason for absences is likely to be illness. Truancy and interviews are more likely to be reasons in the spring and summer terms.

4, 5 You should find that the distribution of $\bar{x}$ for random samples of size 10 is a more compact and symmetrical distribution than that for $\bar{x}$ from random samples of 5. Your results should be close to these.

Size of random samples	Mean of $\bar{x}$	Variance of $\bar{x}$
5	167.4	8.63
10	167.4	4.31

6 Your distribution of sample means will have a mean close to the population mean. The sample means for the samples of $n = 10$ will have a smaller variance than those for $n = 5$.

7 (a) Results for both samples of size 5 and size 10 are likely to be close to the true mean.

(b) A crucial part of the theory underpinning the use of samples is that, as the sample size increases, the distribution of the sample mean becomes increasingly clustered around the true value of the population mean. This is reflected in the smaller variance of the distribution of $\bar{x}$ for samples of size 10 as compared to samples of size 5. The estimates generated by larger random samples are less variable than those generated by smaller random samples so, as you might expect, unusual results from large samples tend to be more significant than those from small samples.

8 (a) You would expect those who regularly commute to the centre to be in favour – also perhaps shop owners.

(b) A total of 48 replied.

(i) 5   (ii) 23   (iii) 20

(c) A sampling procedure ideally should be just as likely to choose one particular member of the population as it is any other, but often this is impracticable.

The sample of 48 were, in fact, the people who filled in a coupon accompanying a previous article on the monorail proposal. Such a sampling procedure is almost bound to introduce bias. In this case, it could be argued that people opposed to new proposals are much more likely to take the trouble to write in than people who feel favourably about them. A better method would be to conduct a random sample of the population of the city and its surrounding districts.

A dictionary might define a bias as a predisposition or prejudice. Thus a die is biased if it is predisposed to show a particular face more than any other. A telephone poll could be predisposed to selecting relatively prosperous members of society.

9 Since no samples in the simulation produced a result as low as five supporting the scheme, it seems highly likely that the actual percentage in support is less than 50%.

10 This shows that, in a poll of 48 people, obtaining 5 or fewer in support of the project is very unlikely. The poll would therefore provide strong evidence that the majority of the population are against the monorail *if* you could be confident that the method of conducting the poll has not introduced bias.

11 A result of 22 is in or near the middle of the distribution: it is the sort of result you would expect if the initial assumption was valid. It would then be quite likely that around 50% of the population were in favour of the monorail.

Exercise C (p. 18)

1 (a) $P(6 \text{ correct}) = \binom{8}{6}\left(\frac{1}{2}\right)^6\left(\frac{1}{2}\right)^2$

$= 28\left(\frac{1}{2}\right)^8$

$= \frac{28}{256} \ (\approx 11\%)$

(b) $P(6 \text{ or more}) = \binom{8}{6}\left(\frac{1}{2}\right)^8 + \binom{8}{7}\left(\frac{1}{2}\right)^8$

$+ \binom{8}{8}\left(\frac{1}{2}\right)^8$

$= \frac{28}{256} + \frac{8}{256} + \frac{1}{256}$

$= \frac{37}{256} \ (\approx 14\%)$

Random guessing would produce a result of 6 or more correct 'predictions' in about 14% of cases. 7 or 8 correct results would have been more convincing.

2 Assuming that the taster cannot tell the difference, and is 50% likely to be correct each time,

P(7 or more correct)

$= \frac{120 + 45 + 10 + 1}{1024} = \frac{176}{1024} \ (\approx 17\%)$

P(8 or more correct)

$= \frac{45 + 10 + 1}{1024} = \frac{56}{1024} \ (\approx 5\%)$

P(9 or more correct)

$= \frac{10 + 1}{1024} = \frac{11}{1024} \ (\approx 1\%)$

8 or more correct is quite convincing. 9 or 10 correct would make you more certain that they are not guessing.

3 (a) For a large number of samples, the coin should come down heads three times or less for about 17% of the time

There is some suspicion of bias but such a result is to be expected about one time out of six.

(b) The chance of an unbiased coin coming down heads thirty times or fewer out of 100 tosses is actually less than 0.01%.

It is therefore reasonable to suspect that the coin is biased.

2   Continuous random variables

A   The uniform or rectangular distribution (p. 20)

1

x	1	2	3	4	5	6
$P(X=x)$	$\frac{1}{6}$	$\frac{1}{6}$	$\frac{1}{6}$	$\frac{1}{6}$	$\frac{1}{6}$	$\frac{1}{6}$

2D   (a)   Area = 1 (representing total probability)

(b) $h = \frac{1}{6}$

Exercise A (p. 21)

2   (a) $\frac{1}{2}$ (b) 0   (c) $\frac{1}{3}$ (d) 0

(e) $\frac{1}{6}$ (f) $\frac{5}{12}$ (g) $\frac{5}{12}$

2   (a) $f(x) = \begin{cases} \frac{1}{4} & -2 \leqslant x < 2 \\ 0 & \text{elsewhere} \end{cases}$

(b) $\frac{1}{4}$ (c) $\frac{5}{8}$

3E   No as $P(X=1) = 0$

B   Some notation (p. 21)

Exercise B (p. 21)

1   (a) 1   (b) $\frac{2}{5}$ (c) $\frac{2}{5}$ (d) $\frac{3}{5}$
(e) $\frac{1}{10}$ (f) 0

2   (a) $\frac{1}{2}$ (b) $\frac{1}{3}$ (c) $\frac{1}{6}$ (d) $\frac{5}{6}$
(e) $\frac{1}{12}$ (f) 0

C   Other probability density functions (p. 22)

1   (a)   The total area = 1

(b)   The graph spans all the possible values of the variable, and the sum of the probabilities of all the possible values occurring is 1.

Exercise C (p. 23)

1   (a) $\frac{1}{2}$ (b) $\frac{1}{8}$ (c) $\frac{3}{4}$ (d) 0

2   (a)   Area under graph is 1.

(b) $\int_{0}^{1} \frac{1}{2} x \, dx = \left[\frac{x^2}{4}\right]_{0}^{1} = \frac{1}{4}$

(c) $\int_{\frac{1}{2}}^{2} \frac{1}{2} x \, dx = \left[\frac{x^2}{4}\right]_{\frac{1}{2}}^{2} = 1 - \frac{1}{16} = \frac{15}{16}$

(d) $\int_{\frac{1}{2}}^{1\frac{1}{2}} \frac{1}{2} x \, dx = \left[\frac{x^2}{4}\right]_{\frac{1}{2}}^{1\frac{1}{2}} = \frac{2.25}{4} - \frac{0.25}{4} = \frac{1}{2}$

3   (a)

(b)   0

(c) $P(1 \leqslant x \leqslant 3\frac{1}{2}) = \frac{1}{4} + \frac{1}{2} + \left(\frac{\frac{1}{2} + \frac{1}{4}}{2}\right) \times \frac{1}{2}$

$= \frac{1}{4} + \frac{1}{2} + \frac{3}{16} = \frac{15}{16}$

(d) $P(x \geqslant 2\frac{1}{2}) = \frac{1}{4} + \frac{1}{4} = \frac{1}{2}$

4   (a)   Area $= \frac{1}{2} \times 1 \times h + 2h = 1$

$2.5h = 1$

So $h = \frac{1}{2.5} = 0.4$

(b) $g(x) = \begin{cases} 0.4x & 0 \leqslant x \leqslant 1 \\ 0.4 & 1 \leqslant x \leqslant 3 \\ 0 & \text{elsewhere} \end{cases}$

(c)   (i)

$P(0.5 \leqslant X \leqslant 2.5) = \left(\frac{0.2 + 0.4}{2}\right) \times \frac{1}{2}$

$+ 0.4 \times 1.5$

$= 0.15 + 0.6 = 0.75$

(ii) $P(X < 2) = 0.2 + 0.4 = 0.6$

3 The Normal distribution

A Variability (p. 25)

1D From a sample of 100 adult males you would expect a histogram shaped like the one below.

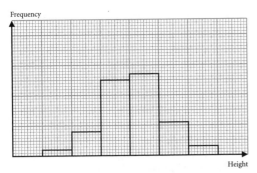

There are few men who are **very** tall or **very** short. Most men are somewhere in the middle.

2 (a)

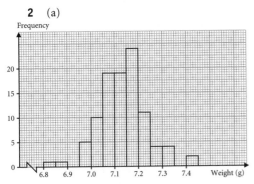

(b) Your calculation of the mean and standard deviation.

(c) (i) ±1 s.d. covers approximately the range of values 7.03 to 7.23. There are about 70% of the observations within ±1 s.d. of the mean.

  (ii) You are looking for values below 6.93 and above 7.33 (approximately). There are about 8% of the observations more than 2 s.d. from the mean.

3 (a)

Data set A

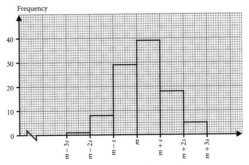

Data set B

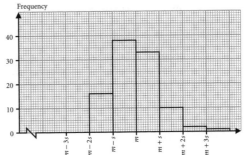

Data set C

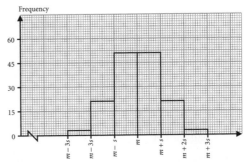

Data set D

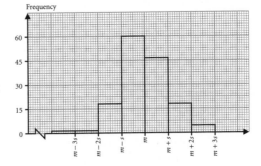

Data set E

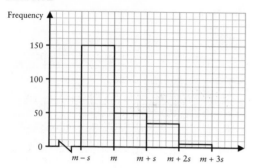

(b) Approximately,
(i) 70%   (ii) 15%   (iii) 0%
(except for data set E, see part (c))

(c) Approximate proportion of
observations within n standard
deviations of the mean

	±1	±2	±3	Beyond 3
A	0.68	0.94	1	0
B	0.71	0.97	0.99	0.01
C	0.68	0.96	1	0
D	0.71	0.96	0.99	0.01
E	0.80	0.92	0.98	0.02

4D The distributions are similar in shape, the
only exception being data set E. Data sets
A, B, C and D have similar proportions of
values within ±1 s.d., ±2 s.d., ±3 s.d. of the
mean. When compared with the
distribution of the weights of coins you
should find that A, B, C and D are
remarkably similar and only set E is the
odd one out.

5D You cannot say which was the better result
without some other information, such as
the spread of marks. Although her score in
economics is higher, everyone may have
scored highly in economics, whereas her
mathematics result might have been
among the best in the class.

6 Other data sets will produce the same
results for the mean and the standard
deviation. In each case the mean of
standardised data is 0 and the standard
deviation is 1, although rounding errors in
the calculations will lead only
approximately to these values.

Exercise A (p. 32)

1 (a) −1   (b) −2.833   (c) 1   (d) $\dfrac{x-m}{d}$

2 (a)

	Standardised scores	
	Mathematics	Economics
Karen	0.833	0.375
Soujit	−2.708	−3.375
Melanie	0	0
Chris	−7.083	−5.375

(b) Mathematics 64 (2.08 standardised),
Economics $\dfrac{x-68}{8} = 2.08 \Rightarrow x \approx 85$

(c) $\dfrac{x-54}{4.8} = \dfrac{x-68}{8} \Rightarrow x = 33$

3 (a) The man is relatively taller:

Male: $\dfrac{-1}{2.8} = -0.36$;

Female: $\dfrac{-1}{2.4} = -0.42$

(b) 5 ft 9 in

4E Let the original observations be
$x_1, x_2, \ldots, x_n$
(mean $= \bar{x}$, s.d. $= s$).

$$z_1 = \frac{x_1 - \bar{x}}{s}, \quad z_2 = \frac{x_2 - \bar{x}}{s}, \ldots$$

$$\bar{z} = \sum_{i=1}^{n}\left(\frac{x_i - \bar{x}}{s}\right) = \frac{1}{s}\sum(x_i - \bar{x})$$

$$= \frac{1}{s}\left(\sum x_i - n\bar{x}\right)$$

But $\sum x_i = n\bar{x}$

So $\bar{z} = 0$

$$V(z) = \frac{1}{n}\sum z_i^2 - (\bar{z})^2$$

$$= \frac{1}{n}\sum z_i^2$$

$$= \frac{1}{n}\sum\left(\frac{x_i - \bar{x}}{s}\right)^2$$

$$= \frac{1}{ns^2}\sum(x_i^2 - 2x_i\bar{x} + (\bar{x})^2)$$

$$= \frac{1}{ns^2}\left(\sum x_i^2 - 2\bar{x}\sum x_i + n(\bar{x})^2\right)$$

$$= \frac{1}{ns^2}\left(\sum x_i^2 - n(\bar{x})^2\right)$$

$$= \frac{1}{ns^2}(ns^2) = 1$$

B   Considering the area (p. 33)

1D   (a)   The area of each block represents frequency in the corresponding interval, i.e. 8, 29, 46, 12 and 5.

   (b)   The total area of all the blocks represents the frequency or total number of values, i.e. 100.

2D   (a)   The total relative frequency is 1 and will always be so for any data set.

   (b)   The area of each block is:

   height of block × width
   = relative frequency for the block

   The total area of the histogram is the sum of the areas of the separate blocks, which is the same as the sum of the relative frequencies. The area of a relative frequency density histogram is therefore 1.

   (c)   The relative frequency density histograms will be similar to those you obtained in question 3 on p. 26 but with different vertical scales. For example:

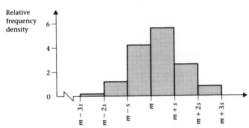

3D   The curve is symmetrical about the mean, 0, and the area under the curve is equal to 1. About $\frac{2}{3}$ of all observations are within 1 standard deviation of the mean. About 95% of all observations are within 2 standard deviations. Observations more than 3 standard deviations from the mean are very unlikely.

4D   (a)

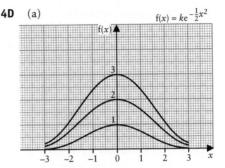

$$f(x) = ke^{-\frac{1}{2}x^2}$$

   Graphs of the functions $e^{-\frac{1}{2}x^2}$, $2e^{-\frac{1}{2}x^2}$, and $3e^{-\frac{1}{2}x^2}$ are shown and clearly display the basic shape that is required.

   If k is negative, then the graphs obtained are mirror images of those shown with a positive value for k. Therefore k must be positive.

   (b)   The area under the curve should be 1. This idea can be used to find k by plotting $f(x)$ for different values of k and obtaining the total area under each curve using, say, the trapezium rule. You can keep adjusting k until the area is (approximately) 1.

5   (a)   The area under $g(x) = e^{-\frac{1}{2}x^2}$ is approximately 2.5 (to 2 s.f.).

   (b)   (i)   about 0.34 (34%)

   (ii)   about 0.14 (14%)

   (iii)   about 0.02 (2%)

   (c)   (i)   0.34

   (ii)   0.14

   (iii)   0.02

6   The proportions are very similar to those for each data set A–D. The differences are partly due to approximations in obtaining the area and, more importantly, because the data sets are samples of only 100 values.

7   Values of k around 0.4 give an area of approximately 1.

8D If approximately 70% of the weights lie within ±1 standard deviation of the mean, then by using the symmetry property of the curve, approximately 35% of the weights will lie between the mean (60 g) and +1 standard deviation (75 g).

Exercise B (p. 38)

1 Your values should be, approximately:

a	b	Area
0	1	0.341
1	2	0.136
2	3	0.0215

2 The area between ±1 s.d. is 0.682.
The area between ±2 s.d. is 0.954.
The area between ±3 s.d. is 0.997.

3 (a) 0.68   (b) 0.046   (c) 0.001

C   Tables for the Normal function (p. 39)

1D
$$P(z > 2) = 0.023$$
$$P(0 < z < 2) = 0.477$$
$$P(-2 < z < 0) = 0.477$$
$$P(z < -2) = 0.023$$
$$P(-2 < z < 2) = 0.954$$
$$P(|z| > 2) = 0.046 \text{ etc.}$$

Exercise C (p. 42)

1 (a) 0.092

(b)
(i) 0.067   (ii) 0.977

(c)
(i) 0.947   (ii) 0.929   (iii) 0.055

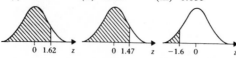

(d)
(i) 0.045   (ii) 0.775   (iii) 0.242

2 (a) 0.683   (b) 0.954   (c) 0.997

3 (a) $z = 1.22$
(b) $z = 0.44$
(c) $z = 1.50$
(d) $z = -0.04$
(e) $z = -1.15$

4 (a) $z = -1.52$
(b) $z = -1.18$
(c) $z = 0.77$
(d) $z = 0.35$
(e) $z = -0.07$

D   Solving problems (p. 43)

1D As 166 cm is approximately 1 standard deviation above the mean, you could expect approximately 16% of women to have a height greater than 166 cm.

Exercise D (answers p. 45)

1 $z = \dfrac{132 - 100}{15} = 2.133$ $\Phi(2.133) = 0.983$
(to 3 s.f.)

The percentage with an IQ of 132 or more is 1.7%.

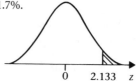

2 $z = \dfrac{1.52 - 1.5}{0.01} = 2$ $\Phi(2) = 0.9772$

The proportion rejected as being over 1.52 cm is 2.3%

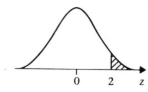

3 $1 - \Phi(z) = 0.97$ $z = -1.88$

$$-1.88 = \frac{1 - m}{0.0025}$$

The mean must be 1.005 kg.

4 $\Phi(z) = 0.005$ $z = -2.575$

$$\frac{1.5 - 1.53}{\sigma} = -2.575$$

The standard deviation must be 0.0117 kg.

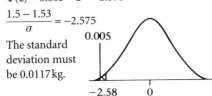

5 $\Phi(z) = 0.7$ $z = 0.524$

$$\frac{78 - 68}{\sigma} = 0.524$$

The standard deviation is 19.08.

6 $\Phi(z) = 0.75$ $z = 0.675$

$$\frac{31 - 28}{\sigma} = 0.675$$

The standard deviation must be 4.44 days.

7 $\dfrac{498.5 - 500}{4} < z < \dfrac{500.5 - 500}{4}$

$-0.375 < z < 0.125$

19.6% of tubs will weigh between 498.5 g and 500.5 g.

8 $\dfrac{150 - 154.2}{5.1} < z < \dfrac{155 - 154.2}{5.1}$

$-0.824 < z < 0.157$

35.7% of the girls are between 150 cm and 155 cm tall.

9 $\Phi(z) = 0.9$ $z = 1.28$

$$\frac{70 - \mu}{\sigma} = 1.28$$

$\Phi(z) = 0.2$ $z = -0.84$

$$\frac{35 - \mu}{\sigma} = -0.84$$

The mean is 48.87 and the standard deviation is 16.51.

4 Data collection

A Data, data everywhere! (p. 47)

1D Examples of variations you could consider are:

- to use 3 jars with 50 tadpoles in each
- to use 150 jars with 1 tadpole in each
- to use 15 jars with 10 tadpoles in each.

The discussion could consider general issues. For example, how many thermostats are there? How much laboratory space is there? Might 50 tadpoles suffer from overcrowding?

More technical issues can also be mentioned. For instance, in the third variation what is the sample size? Is it 15 (jars) or 150 (tadpoles)?

If a similar study has been conducted in previous years, there may be data available that could help you to choose the design.

You could question the basis of the study. Tadpoles do not normally live in thermostatically controlled jars in a laboratory, so how realistic is the whole study? Why not study tadpoles in their natural habitat?

It is not really possible to control the temperature in a pond, but you could find a number of ponds with tadpoles. In each pond you could record both the growth rate and the temperature. Would this be better? Would there be any practical or conceptual problems?

The first type of study is an experiment, while the second is a survey.

2D (a) A survey gives the opportunity to collect and analyse data from a large sample relatively quickly. (You do not have to wait during the nine months of a full-term pregnancy!)

(b) The purpose of the study is presumably to find out if a change in behaviour is advisable. It may therefore be particularly important to study the effect, for habitual smokers, of not smoking during pregnancy. You might therefore carry out an experiment with two groups of smokers. The members of one group are helped and encouraged to give up smoking during their pregnancies and their success in doing this must be carefully monitored.

You may have thought of a number of other possibilities. Whether you use a survey or an experiment, it is important to note that weights at birth are very variable whether or not the mothers smoke during pregnancy.

B Survey methods (p. 49)

1 This is an interesting way of collecting information and it is almost certainly the case that had those buying the books been asked directly (perhaps one month after the purchase) if they had read the book, the results might have been different! The designers had taken a number of precautions (hiding the coupon, paying money to callers, allowing sufficient time for them to telephone) so why was there such a low response?

Some points which could be made about this survey are as follows.

- This was not actually a survey to see whether people read the books but whether they read them within a month.

- The £5 incentive might not be sufficient.

In the family expenditure survey of 1967, payment was made for co-operation on the part of a household and yet 29% did not respond. There are other examples of non-response for national surveys involving payment to respondents. It is therefore not clear whether most people did not read the books within a month or whether they read them but did not bother to claim the £5.

2D They would first need to be clear about the sort of information they require. They might want to know for example:

- who would use the centre and for what purpose

- how frequently they would use it

- at what times they would use it

- how much they would be prepared to pay

- how they would travel to the sports centre.

You doubtless can think of other issues.

To obtain valid information about requirements they would need to take care to ask people across the full age range. It would be important to record the age and sex of the respondent as this would provide useful information. Using a questionnaire would be the best way of obtaining the information – perhaps by interviewing people in person, or by telephone, rather than posting out forms.

If the sampling method used was to ask every tenth person in a shopping arcade on a Saturday afternoon then some points of view could be disproportionately represented.

3D (a) For each area you must obtain the number of trees and the number of large trees. A quick and easy method is needed to define what is meant by 'large' – a common method is to use a special tape to measure the diameter of the tree at chest height. It is conventional to describe a pine with a diameter of more than 30 cm as large. The Forestry Commission plants all its commercial forests in straight lines and so counting is relatively easy.

The 14 areas must be chosen at random. You might, for example, number each area and use random numbers to select 14 numbers from 1 to 168.

(b) Without some experience of similar sampling exercises, you cannot tell whether a sample of 14 areas will be sufficient. Organisations conducting sampling procedures usually have a clear idea how large a sample needs to be in order for it to be reliable.

4 You must ensure that **every** number has an equal chance of being selected. Using a computer or calculator is the easiest way of generating the numbers. Most devices have a simple means of generating a whole number from 1 to N, for any N. You must repeat this until you have obtained 14 **different** numbers.

This straightforward method is efficient because 14 is very much smaller than 168 and so you are unlikely to need to repeat the procedure much more than 14 times.

5 Your table should record the plot number, the numbers of small and large trees and the total number of trees on the plot.

6 Typical results for scheme A are as shown.

Plot number	Small trees	Large trees	Total
15	74	127	201
16	78	135	213
27	71	121	192
30	78	113	191
32	107	147	254
40	85	137	222
63	86	128	214
69	91	139	230
81	100	222	322
88	90	221	311
108	110	238	348
127	107	205	312
166	104	189	293
167	107	238	345
Mean	92	168.6	260.6

The estimates are:
- the number of trees on the whole plot is $168 \times 260.6 \approx 43\,800$
- the number of large trees is $168 \times 168.6 \approx 28\,300$
- the proportion of large trees is $\dfrac{28\,300}{43\,800} \approx 0.65$.

7 $6:8$ is the same ratio as $72:96$.

8 Tables similar to the one for question 6 should be used.

9 Typical results for scheme B are as shown.

Plot number	Small trees	Large trees	Total
Region 1			
23	87	134	221
48	76	122	198
56	89	144	233
57	94	136	230
71	79	123	202
72	93	149	242
Mean	86.3	134.7	221.0
Region 2			
74	91	189	280
80	95	233	328
84	106	242	348
89	107	222	329
116	94	196	290
119	121	258	379
139	100	240	340
141	105	228	333
Mean	102.4	226.0	328.4

An estimate for the total number of trees on the plot is
$$72 \times 221 + 96 \times 328.4 \approx 47\,400.$$

A similar estimate for the number of large trees is $72 \times 134.7 + 96 \times 226 \approx 31\,400$.

The proportion is therefore $\dfrac{31\,400}{47\,400} \approx 0.66$.

10 For the samples above, the variances of the total number of trees on each plot are:

Region 1   259 (to 3 s.f.)
Region 2   865 (to 3 s.f.)

There is a much greater variation in the number of trees per plot in Region 2 than in Region 1. An estimate based on a sample from Region 1 is therefore likely to be more reliable than an estimate based on a sample from Region 2. It would therefore be a good idea to sample Region 2 more intensely, to produce an estimate of which one can be more confident.

If it is known there there is little variability, then repeated sampling provides more of the same information. To illustrate the point further, if a stratum consisted of identical elements (no variability) then just one sample would provide the information you need.

11   If you choose, for example, 2♥ and K♣ then your estimate of the mean score would be $\frac{2+10}{2} = 6$. This is reasonably close to 7, although your estimate could be as low as 2 or as high as 10.

12   The stick graph given was obtained by doing the experiment. Yours is likely to be similar in that the estimates will be only loosely grouped around 7.

13   In this case, the lowest possible estimate you could have is $\frac{2+8}{2} = 5$ and the highest possible estimate is $\frac{7+10}{2} = 8.5$.

14   The following graph was obtained by using the method.

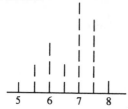

A comparison between this stick graph and the one in question 12 suggests strongly that an estimate based upon the stratified sampling procedure is likely to have greater precision than one based upon the simple random sampling procedure. Your results (and those of others in your group) should also lead to this conclusion.

15E From your computer simulation you should find that larger samples lead to greater precision, as does sampling more intensely from the stratum of low cards. Note that if you employ a stratified sampling scheme using 3 cards from the low value pack and one from the high value pack, then samples such as {3♥, 4♠, 7♣} and {9♦} lead to an estimate for the mean of

$$\frac{3+4+7+3\times9}{6} \approx 6.8$$

16D Some ways of dividing the population into strata whose spending behaviours are likely to differ greatly are as follows:

- by gender
- by whether or not the person lives at home
- by whether the person is employed, unemployed or a student.

You may have thought of several other good ways of stratifying the population.

17D The voting behaviour of many people is reasonably stable. Consequently, it is important to focus attention on new voters and those who are prone to change allegiance (the 'floating' voters).

At each general election, those eligible to vote for the first time can span up to 5 years of the age range of the population. This stratum therefore comprises a large number of people whose voting intentions (and indeed whether they vote at all) can significantly affect the result. Whilst the connection between party allegiance and social class is far from straightforward, the simple division between 'working-class' and 'middle-class' still provides probably the clearest division of the electorate into strata with dissimilar voting intentions. The growth in the numbers of white collar workers is one of the major factors which blurs this distinction and so the intentions of this stratum have special importance.

Focussing on various strata of the electorate whose intentions you believe to be more volatile is just one example of the use of stratified sampling. A similar idea is employed when pollsters concentrate on the key marginals – those constituencies which are most likely to change hands.

C Questionnaire design (p. 56)

1D Some of the features you may have commented on are as follows:

- The questionnaire starts with a brief and simple explanation of the purpose of the research in a way which will encourage the respondent to take the time to complete the form.

- Respondents are directed away from questions (like numbers 4 and 5) if they are not relevant.

- The questions are intended to be clearly worded and simple to answer.

- A very important feature is the way respondents only need to tick boxes. This idea is covered in more depth in the next discussion point.

2D (a) 'Where do you usually buy milk?'

(b) **Open response**

Some advantages are:

- respondents think more deeply about their answers

- information may become available which the interviewer had not anticipated.

Some disadvantages are:

- an interviewer has to decide whether to record everything said, record relevant remarks or paraphrase the answers

- an interviewer's interpretation of an answer may introduce bias

- answers have to be encoded before the data can be analysed

- respondents may find the task so time-consuming that they fail to complete the questionnaire.

Closed response

Some advantages are:

- it is simple to answer such a question

- little thought or analysis is needed by the respondent.

Some disadvantages are:

- answers may be forced into categories in which they do not really belong

- a reply may be wrongly recorded by ticking the wrong box

- respondents do not think deeply enough about their replies but may just tick a box. (Some questionnaires are designed with questions repeated using a different form of words. This provides a check on whether a respondent's answers are reliable.)

(c) Question 2 has been designed to be 'closed response' and simple to answer for most respondents. Notice also that the possibility of 'one or more' ticks has been highlighted.

Less common answers are catered for by allowing an 'open response' answer if necessary.

3D **Advantages**

- Results can be obtained very quickly.

- It is especially suitable if the questions are simple and straightforward and do not require much thought.

Disadvantages

- Bias has immediately been introduced because not everyone has a telephone.

- Special care must be taken regarding who is allowed to answer the questions. The person in whose name the telephone is registered is very often male.

5 From binomial to Normal

A Finding probabilities (p. 59)

1D It looks similar to the bell shape of the Normal distribution. This similarity will be explained in this chapter.

2D For values of p approximately equal to 0.5 the distribution is approximately symmetrical and bell-shaped. For large (near 1) or small (near 0) values of p you can still obtain the bell shape by increasing n.

3D   A discrete random variable can take only certain distinct values, such as the number of children in a family or the number of cars passing a particular junction. A continuous random variable can take any value within a given range, for example the heights of all sixth-form pupils, or the length of time shoppers have to wait at the supermarket check-out.

4D   (a) For $X \sim B(60, \frac{1}{6})$ the probability of winning the car is

$$P(X = 30) + P(X = 31) + \cdots + P(X = 60)$$

$$P(X = 30) = \binom{60}{30}\left(\frac{1}{6}\right)^{30}\left(\frac{5}{6}\right)^{30} \approx 2 \times 10^{-9}$$

The other probabilities are even less likely and the total probability of winning the car is actually less than 10^{-8}.

Winning once in 10^{8} turns would cost you $10^{8} \times 10p$ or £10 million. It would be much better to buy a car!

(b) Obtaining 20 or more sixes is slightly more likely.

$$P(X = 20, 21, 22, ..., 60)$$

$$= \binom{60}{20}\left(\frac{1}{6}\right)^{20}\left(\frac{5}{6}\right)^{40} + \binom{60}{21}\left(\frac{1}{6}\right)^{21}\left(\frac{5}{6}\right)^{39} + \cdots$$

$$\approx 0.001$$

Winning £10 once in every 1000 goes would cost you £100 so, again, it does not seem worth having a turn.

5

n	p	Mean (of B(n, p))	Variance (of B(n, p))	Standard deviation (of B(n, p))
10	$\frac{1}{2}$	5	2.5	1.58
20	$\frac{1}{2}$	10	5	2.24
20	$\frac{1}{4}$	5	3.75	1.94
40	$\frac{1}{2}$	20	10	3.16
40	$\frac{1}{4}$	10	7.5	2.74
100	$\frac{1}{2}$	50	25	5.00

6   Mean $= n \times p$

7   Variance $= np(1 - p)$
        or npq where $q = 1 - p$

8   Standard deviation $= \sqrt{\text{variance}}$
        $= \sqrt{(np(1 - p))}$
        or $\sqrt{npq}$

9   The number of heads $X \sim B(1000, 0.5)$

A Normal distribution with mean $= np = 500$ and variance $= npq = 250$ would model this distribution.

530 is **about** 2 standard deviations above the mean:

$\Phi(2) = 0.977$ (from tables)

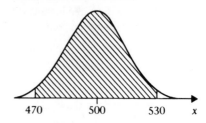

So there is a probability of approximately 95% that there will be between 470 and 530 heads. About 95% of the throws of 1000 coins would result in between 470 and 530 heads. You would be very unlikely to obtain a number of heads outside this range.

10   The Normal distribution would have

mean $= np = 12$

variance $= npq = 9$

So B($48, \frac{1}{4}$) is approximately N(12, 9).

11   Since the total area must be 1, the area to the right must be 1 minus the area to the left.

Exercise A (p. 65)

1 (a) B$(100, \frac{1}{2})$ is approximated by
        N$(50, 25)$. P$(X \geqslant 52)$ is the area to the
        right of 51.5.

$$z = \frac{51.5 - 50}{5} = 0.3$$

        P$(Z > 0.3) = 0.382$

   (b) B$(1000, \frac{1}{2})$ is approximated by
        N$(500, 250)$. P$(X \geqslant 520)$ is the area to
        the right of 519.5.

$$z = \frac{519.5 - 500}{\sqrt{250}} = 1.233$$

        P$(Z > 1.233) = 0.109$

   (c) B$(10\,000, \frac{1}{2})$ is approximated by
        N$(5000, 2500)$. P$(X \geqslant 5200)$ is the
        area to the right of 5199.5.

$$z = \frac{5199.5 - 5000}{50} = 3.99$$

        P$(Z > 3.99) = 0.000$

2 B$(220, 0.7)$ is approximated by
     N$(140, 42)$.

$$z = \frac{149.5 - 140}{\sqrt{42}} = 1.466$$

     P$(Z > 1.466) = 0.071$

3 B$(30, \frac{1}{6})$ is approximated by N$(5, 4.167)$.
     P$(X = 5)$ is the area between 4.5 and 5.5.

$$z = \frac{5.5 - 5}{\sqrt{4.167}} = 0.245$$

$$z = \frac{4.5 - 5}{\sqrt{4.167}} = -0.245$$

     P$(-0.245 < Z < 0.245) = 0.194$

4 B$(1000, 0.02)$ is approximated by
     N$(20, 19.6)$.

$$z = \frac{20.5 - 20}{\sqrt{19.6}} = 0.1129$$

     P$(Z > 0.1129) = 0.455$

5 B$(1000, 0.15)$ is approximated by
     N$(150, 127.5)$.

   (a) P$(X < 130)$ is the area to the left of
        129.5.

$$z = \frac{129.5 - 150}{\sqrt{127.5}} = -1.816$$

        P$(Z < -1.816) = 0.035$

   (b) P$(140 < X < 155)$ is the area between
        140.5 and 154.5.

$$z = \frac{140.5 - 150}{\sqrt{127.5}} = -0.841$$

$$z = \frac{154.5 - 150}{\sqrt{127.5}} = 0.399$$

        P$(-0.841 < X < 0.399) = 0.455$

6 B$(75, 0.8)$ is approximated by N$(60, 12)$.
     P$(X > 65)$ is the area to the right of 65.5.

$$z = \frac{65.5 - 60}{\sqrt{12}} = 1.588$$

     P$(Z > 1.588) = 0.0561$

7 B$(250, 0.24)$ is approximated by
     N$(60, 45.6)$.

     P$(X < 55)$ is the area to the left of 54.5.

$$z = \frac{54.5 - 60}{\sqrt{45.6}} = -0.814$$

     P$(Z < -0.814) = 0.208$

8 B$(160, \frac{3}{5})$ is approximated by N$(96, 38.4)$.
     P$(90 < X < 100)$ is the area between 90.5
     and 99.5.

$$z = \frac{90.5 - 96}{\sqrt{38.4}} = -0.888$$

$$z = \frac{99.5 - 96}{\sqrt{38.4}} = 0.565$$

     P$(-0.888 < Z < 0.565) = 0.527$

9   B(200, 0.11) is approximated by
N(22, 19.58).

(a) P(X< 20) is the area to the left of
19.5.

$$z = \frac{19.5 - 22}{\sqrt{19.58}} = -0.565$$

P(Z < −0.565) = 0.286

(b) P(20 < X< 30) is the area between
20.5 and 29.5.

$$z = \frac{20.5 - 22}{\sqrt{19.58}} = -0.339$$

$$z = \frac{29.5 - 22}{\sqrt{19.58}} = 1.695$$

P(−0.339 < Z< 1.695) = 0.588

10   Men: B(250, 0.186) is approximated by
N(46.5, 37.851).

P(X> 50) is the area to the right of 50.5.

$$z = \frac{50.5 - 46.5}{\sqrt{37.851}} = -0.650$$

P(Z > −0.650) = 0.258

Women: B(300, 0.189) is approximated by
N(56.7, 45.984).

P(50 < X< 60) is the area between 50.5
and 59.5.

$$z = \frac{50.5 - 56.7}{\sqrt{45.984}} = -0.914$$

$$z = \frac{59.5 - 56.7}{\sqrt{45.984}} = 0.413$$

P(−0.914 < Z< 0.413) = 0.480

6   Estimating population parameters

A   Sampling distribution of the mean
(p. 67)

1   Your own solution will differ from this
example, which is provided as an
illustration.

Sample mean weight (g)	Tally	Frequency
6.80–		0
6.85–		0
6.90–	||	2
6.95–		0
7.00–	|||	3
7.05–	ЖТ ЖТ ||	12
7.10–	ЖТ ЖТ |||	13
7.15–	ЖТ ЖТ ЖТ |	16
7.20–	||	2
7.25–	||	2
7.30–		0
7.35–		0
7.40–		0

For the parent population:

mean = 7.13
variance = 0.010

For the sample of size 2 given above:

mean (of 50 samples) = 7.13

2   Your frequency chart for the distribution
of means.

3   Your mean of the distribution of means.

Your variance of the distribution of means.

4   The mean of the distribution of the sample
means is very close to the population
mean, but the variance of the sample
means is smaller than the population
variance. It is known that the parent
population is Normally distributed.

The frequency chart is likely to suggest
that the distribution of the sample means
is also approximately Normal.

5, 6, 7   You should notice that the means and
standard deviations are similar to the
population mean and standard deviation
in each case – but more reliably so as the
sample size increases.

8 The mean of the sample means should be very close to the population mean (of zero).

The standard deviation of the sample means (called 'standard error') will be approximately $\frac{1}{2}$ of the population standard deviation ($\frac{1}{2}$ when $n = 4$).

Variance of sample means $\approx \frac{1}{4}$ for $n = 4$.

9 For $n = 8$,

$$\mu_{\bar{x}} = 0, \qquad \sigma_{\bar{x}} = \frac{1}{\sqrt{8}}, \qquad \sigma_{\bar{x}}^2 = \frac{1}{8}$$

For $n = 10$,

$$\mu_{\bar{x}} = 0, \qquad \sigma_{\bar{x}} = \frac{1}{\sqrt{10}}, \qquad \sigma_{\bar{x}}^2 = \frac{1}{10}$$

For $n = 20$,

$$\mu_{\bar{x}} = 0, \qquad \sigma_{\bar{x}} = \frac{1}{\sqrt{20}}, \qquad \sigma_{\bar{x}}^2 = \frac{1}{20}$$

10 The graph should be a straight line through the origin.

12D The total of the unshaded areas $= 1 - 0.999 = 0.001$.
The area above $b = 0.0005$ and area below $b = 0.9995$.
From tables

$$\Phi(z) = 0.9995$$
$$z = 3.29$$

13, 14 In each case $\mu_{\bar{x}} = \mu$,

$$\sigma_{\bar{x}} = \frac{\sigma}{\sqrt{n}}, \qquad \sigma_{\bar{x}}^2 = \frac{\sigma^2}{n}$$

where $n = 4, 8, 10, 20$.

15 The graph should be a straight line through the origin.

16 Your own check.

17 The same results are found.

Exercise A (p. 74)

1 $X \sim N(166, 6^2)$

Sample size 5, $\bar{X} \sim N\left(166, \frac{6^2}{5}\right)$

$z = 1.49$

$P(-1.49 < Z < 1.49) = 0.864$

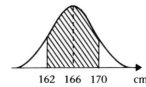

Sample size 8, $\bar{X} \sim N\left(166, \frac{6^2}{8}\right)$

$z = 1.886$

$P(-1.886 < Z < 1.886) = 0.941$

2 $X \sim N(980, 120^2)$

Sample size 10, $\bar{X} \sim N\left(980, \frac{120^2}{10}\right)$

(a) $P(970 < \bar{X} < 1010)$
$= P(-0.264 < Z < 0.791) = 0.39$

(b) $P(950 < \bar{X} < 1030)$
$= P(-0.791 < Z < 1.318) = 0.69$

(c) $P(940 < \bar{X} < 1040)$
$= P(-1.054 < Z < 1.581) = 0.80$

3 $X \sim N(162, 3.5^2)$

Sample size n, $\bar{X} \sim N\left(162, \frac{3.5^2}{n}\right)$

(a) $\dfrac{163.5 - 162}{3.5/\sqrt{n}} = 1.96$

$n = 20.9$

A sample of size 21 must be taken.

(b) A sample of 48 must be taken.

4 (a) 26 (b) 234

5 0.030

6 (a) 0.401 (b) 0.193

B Estimating with confidence (p. 75)

1D (a) In Section A you saw that the distribution of sample means has the same mean as the population. So, if Class 5 continued taking samples of 25 jars of water, you would expect all their various values for the pH to average out at the actual mean pH of the river. The single value they obtained is therefore called an **unbiased estimator** of the population mean. You have also seen that, the larger the sample size, the more tightly clustered is the distribution of possible sample means. An estimate based upon a sample mean is therefore more reliable when the sample size is large.

(b) The mean pH values for the water from Clean Valley, as calculated by two groups, fall within EU guidelines, although the value obtained by the environmental group lies outside the recommended range. This value was based on a smaller sample (5 samples) and is therefore less reliable.

Care must be taken when considering results obtained by groups which have particular interests. In this instance, a large sample obtained by an independent group would be necessary.

2D The 12 samples which give mean values tightly bunched between 7.5 and 8.5 are more likely to indicate the actual pH level of the water. There is less variation in these results, which suggests that they are probably more accurate.

The other set of results has mean values more widely spread and you should feel less confident about using these to predict the actual pH value.

3 Clean Valley Primary School:

$n = 25,$ variance of $\bar{x} = \dfrac{0.5}{n} = 0.02$

$\bar{x} = 8.5$ $(n = 25,$ s.e. $= \sqrt{0.02} = 0.141)$

Clean Valley Water Authority:

$n = 100,$ variance of $\bar{x} = \dfrac{0.5}{n} = 0.005$

$\bar{x} = 8.3$ $(n = 100,$ s.e. $= \sqrt{0.005} = 0.071)$

Exercise B (p. 77)

1 (a) 0.4 (b) 0.095

2 (a) $\bar{x} = 5.57, n = 6,$ s.e. $= 0.816$

(b) $\bar{x} = 6.75, n = 20,$ s.e. $= 0.447$

3 $\bar{x} = 3.7, n = 40,$ s.e. $= 0.079$

3 s.e. above the mean would give a value of 3.94.

This is still well below the normal pH of 5.7, which suggests that there is excess acid in the rain.

C Confidence intervals (p. 77)

1D The distribution of sample means is Normal. You know from earlier work that approximately 68% of all possible values lie within 1 standard deviation of the mean value.

2D The confidence interval gets wider. You can say with certainty, for example, that the height of adult females in England is between 0 and 500 cm!

3D Approximately 95% of sample means fall within two standard errors of the population mean. The figure taken from the Normal tables is in fact 95.4%. To be more confident of providing an interval estimate that contains the true population mean, you would simply quote a wider confidence interval.

4 (a) Clean Valley Primary School:

$\bar{x} = 8.15, n = 25, \sigma^2 = 0.5$

s.e. $= \dfrac{\sigma}{\sqrt{n}} = 0.141$

68% confidence interval $(8.01, 8.29)$
95% confidence interval $(7.87, 8.43)$

(b) Clean Valley Water Authority:

$\bar{x} = 7.8, n = 100, \sigma^2 = 0.5$

s.e. $= \dfrac{\sigma}{\sqrt{n}} = 0.071$

68% confidence interval $(7.73, 7.87)$
95% confidence interval $(7.66, 7.94)$

5

	68%	95%
(a)	(4.75, 6.39)	(3.94, 7.20)
(b)	(6.30, 7.20)	(5.86, 7.64)

6 $(\bar{x} - 3 \text{ s.e.}, \bar{x} + 3 \text{ s.e.})$ gives a 99.7% confidence interval.

7 $\Phi(z) = 0.95 \Rightarrow z = 1.645$

8 $\Phi(z) = 0.975 \Rightarrow z = 1.96$

Similarly for 99% confidence interval

$\Phi(z) = 0.995$

$\Rightarrow z = 2.58$

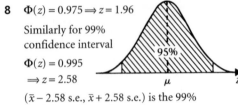

$(\bar{x} - 2.58 \text{ s.e.}, \bar{x} + 2.58 \text{ s.e.})$ is the 99% confidence interval.

Exercise C (p. 80)

1 $n = 9$, $\sigma = 10$, $\bar{x} = 20$, s.e. $= 3.33$

90% confidence interval $(14.52, 25.48)$
95% confidence interval $(13.47, 26.53)$
99% confidence interval $(11.41, 28.59)$

2 The confidence intervals would be smaller.

$n = 25$, $\sigma = 10$, $\bar{x} = 20$, s.e. $= 2$

90% confidence interval $(16.71, 23.29)$
95% confidence interval $(16.08, 23.92)$
99% confidence interval $(14.84, 25.16)$

3 (a) $(12.59, 13.61)$ (b) $(2.53, 2.77)$
(c) $(201.62, 208.38)$

4 (a) $(0.0999, 0.160)$ (b) $(20.51, 21.29)$
(c) $(842.3, 847.7)$

5 Sample: $n = 50$, $\bar{x} = 26$, $\sigma^2 = 6$

s.e. $= \dfrac{\sqrt{6}}{\sqrt{50}} = 0.346$

The 95% confidence interval is
26 ± 1.96 s.e.
i.e. $(25.3, 26.7)$

6 $\sigma = 9.5$, $n = 10$, s.e. $= 3.004$, $\bar{x} = 117.1$

90% confidence interval $(112.16, 122.04)$

7 (a) Width of 95% confidence interval is 3.92.

(b) Width of 95% confidence interval is 2.77.

(c) Width of 95% confidence interval is 1.96.

For a width of 1, a sample of 1537 would have to be taken.

D Populations with unknown variance (p. 81)

1 This can be checked simply by using the statistics functions on your calculator. Alternatively:

x	-1	1
$x - \mu$	-1	1
$(x - \mu)^2$	1	1
$P(X = x)$	$\frac{1}{2}$	$\frac{1}{2}$

$\sigma^2 = 1 \times \frac{1}{2} + 1 \times \frac{1}{2} = 1$

2D (a) Your own explanation.

(b)

Sample	$(-1, -1, -1)$	$(-1, -1, 1)$	$(-1, 1, 1)$	$(1, 1, 1)$
Probability	$\frac{1}{8}$	$\frac{3}{8}$	$\frac{3}{8}$	$\frac{1}{8}$
Sample mean, $\bar{x}$	-1	$-\frac{1}{3}$	$\frac{1}{3}$	1
Sample variance	0	$\frac{8}{9}$	$\frac{8}{9}$	0

(c) For both $n = 2$ and $n = 3$, the distributions of sample means have mean 0, illustrating the fact that $\bar{x}$ is an unbiased estimator of μ.

3 $\frac{1}{4} \times 0 + \frac{3}{4} \times \frac{8}{9} = \frac{2}{3}$

4E $\mu = 47(0.2) + 48(0.6) + 49(0.2)$
$= 48$
$\sigma^2 = 0.2 \times 1^2 + 0.2 \times 1^2$
$= 0.4$

5E $\bar{x} = 48.5$ when one box contains 48 matches and the other box contains 49 matches. The probability of box 1 having 48 and box 2 having 49 is 0.12, as is the probability of box 1 having 49 and box 2 having 48. The the probability that $\bar{x}$ is $48.5 = 2 \times 0.12 = 0.24$.

6E (a) The mean value of the distribution of $\bar{x}$ is

$$47 \times 0.04 + 47.5 \times 0.24 + 48 \times 0.44$$
$$+ 48.5 \times 0.24 + 49 \times 0.04 = 48$$

(b) The mean value of the distribution of s^2 is

$$0 \times 0.44 + 0.25 \times 0.48 + 1 \times 0.08 = 0.2$$

7E For the **rectangular** population, $\mu = 48$, $\sigma^2 = \frac{2}{3}$.

| | Probabilities | | |
	47	48	49
47	$\frac{1}{9}$	$\frac{1}{9}$	$\frac{1}{9}$
48	$\frac{1}{9}$	$\frac{1}{9}$	$\frac{1}{9}$
49	$\frac{1}{9}$	$\frac{1}{9}$	$\frac{1}{9}$

Sample mean, $\bar{x}$:

x	47	47.5	48	48.5	49
$P(\bar{X} = x)$	$\frac{1}{9}$	$\frac{2}{9}$	$\frac{3}{9}$	$\frac{2}{9}$	$\frac{1}{9}$

The mean value of the distribution of $\bar{x}$ is 48.

Sample variance, s^2:

y	0	0.25	1
$P(s^2 = y)$	$\frac{3}{9}$	$\frac{4}{9}$	$\frac{2}{9}$

The mean value of the distribution of s^2 is $\frac{1}{3}$.

For the **asymmetrical** population, $\mu = 47.5$, $\sigma^2 = 0.45$.

| | Probabilities | | |
	47	48	49
47	0.36	0.18	0.06
48	0.18	0.09	0.03
49	0.06	0.03	0.01

Sample mean, $\bar{x}$:

x	47	47.5	48	48.5	49
$P(\bar{X} = x)$	0.36	0.36	0.21	0.06	0.01

The mean value of the distribution of $\bar{x}$ is 47.5.

Sample variance, s^2:

y	0	0.25	1
$P(s^2 = y)$	0.46	0.42	0.12

The mean value of the distribution of s^2 is 0.225.

For the **u-shaped** population, $\mu = 48$, $\sigma^2 = 1$.

| | Probabilities | | |
	47	48	49
47	0.25	0	0.25
48	0	0	0
49	0.25	0	0.25

Sample mean, $\bar{x}$:

x	47	47.5	48	48.5	49
$P(\bar{X} = x)$	0.25	0	0.5	0	0.25

The mean value of the distribution of $\bar{x}$ is 48.

Sample variance, s^2:

y	0	0.25	1
$P(s^2 = y)$	0.5	0	0.5

The mean value of the distribution of s^2 is 0.5.

In all of these populations you will have found that:

● the mean value of the distribution of $\bar{x}$ is μ

● the mean value of the distribution of s^2 is $\frac{1}{2}\sigma^2$.

Exercise D (p. 86)

1 (a) $s^2 = 0.0017,\ \left(\dfrac{n}{n-1}\right)s^2 = 0.0019$

(b) $s^2 = 33.05,\ \left(\dfrac{n}{n-1}\right)s^2 = 36.72$

2 (a) $s^2 = 2.038,\ \left(\dfrac{n}{n-1}\right)s^2 = 2.061$

(b) $s^2 = 1829,\ \left(\dfrac{n}{n-1}\right)s^2 = 1925$

3 Estimate of mean is 1.501
Sample variance $\approx 8.2 \times 10^{-6}$
Estimate of σ^2 is 9.9×10^{-6}

E Using estimated variances (p. 87)

1D You know from the previous chapter that the distribution of the sample mean is Normal whatever the parent population, provided the sample size is large enough.

In the examples you have considered so far, the variance of the population was known. In practice you would not always know the variance of the population and it may be necessary to find an estimate for it.

2D (a) To find the standard error you must know the population standard deviation.

(b) You do not know the value of the population standard deviation.

You have seen that $\dfrac{ns^2}{n-1}$ is an unbiased estimator of the population variance and this could be used instead of the unknown value.

(c) If the sample size is large enough then the distribution of mean remission times will be Normal, whatever the distribution of the parent population.

3 $n = 29$, $\bar{x} = 13.59$, $s_n^2 = 8.826^2$, $s_{n-1}^2 = 8.982^2$
(a) 95% confidence interval

$$\left(13.59 - 1.96\left(\frac{8.826}{\sqrt{29}}\right), \ 13.59 + 1.96\left(\frac{8.826}{\sqrt{29}}\right)\right)$$

$= (10.38, 16.80)$

(b) 95% confidence interval

$$\left(13.59 - 1.96\left(\frac{8.982}{\sqrt{29}}\right), \ 13.59 + 1.96\left(\frac{8.982}{\sqrt{29}}\right)\right)$$

$= (10.32, 16.86)$

Exercise E (p. 88)

1 (a) Population variance (estimated)

$$= \frac{n}{n-1} s_n^2 = \frac{36}{35} \times 4 = 411$$

A 95% interval is $10 \pm 1.96\,\text{s.e.}$

$$= 10 \pm 1.96\,\frac{\sigma}{\sqrt{n}}$$

$$= 10 \pm 1.96 \times 0.338$$

$$= (9.34, 10.7) \text{ to 3 s.f.}$$

(b) $(19.4, 20.6)$ to 3 s.f.

(c) $(19.9, 20.1)$ to 3 s.f.

The answer is likely to be inaccurate because the sample size is small.

2 $n = 59$, $\bar{x} = 114$, $s_{n-1} = 4.14$, s.e. $= 0.538$
A 90% confidence interval is $(113, 115)$ to 3 s.f.

3 $n = 891$, $\bar{x} = 3.856$, $s_{n-1} = 1.286$, s.e. $= 0.043$
A 95% confidence interval is $(3.77, 3.94)$.

The actual mean age of the fish is unknown. However, this single sample provides an interval which you can be confident contains the mean: if you took a large number of samples of this size, even though *each* would generate *its own* confidence interval for the mean, in 95% of cases you could expect that confidence interval to contain the true mean.

4 (a) $n = 10$, $\bar{x} = 10$, $s_{n-1} = 4.22$, s.e. $= 1.33$
A 90% confidence interval is $(7.8, 12.2)$.

(b) The sample is small, so you can only say that the distribution of sample means is approximately Normal.

F Population proportions (p. 89)

1D If you assume that the marked fish have mixed freely with others in the lake and that the recapture of 40 fish is a random sample of fish in the lake, then the proportion of marked fish in the catch is an estimate of the proportion of marked fish in the lake:

i.e.

$$\frac{5}{40} = \frac{5}{N} \text{ where } N \text{ is the number of fish in the lake.}$$

The estimate of N (based on this information) is 400.

It is likely that the estimates would vary considerably from sample to sample and it is likely that repeated sampling would be necessary to improve confidence in any estimate of the population. In reality, of course, this may not be possible.

It would be interesting if you could discuss how such problems are actually dealt with, perhaps by using examples from biology or geography. You might find out, for example, how population sizes of rare species such as whales are obtained.

2 The number of coloured tiles in your sample of 25 will, of course, vary from sample to sample. If there are x coloured tiles in your sample, then the only estimate you can make for the proportion of coloured tiles in the bag is $\frac{x}{25}$.

If n coloured tiles were placed in the bag so that there were N tiles altogether then

$$\frac{x}{25} \text{ is your estimate of } \frac{n}{N}$$

and your estimate of the number of tiles N in the bag will be

$$N = \frac{25n}{x}$$

The mean value of your estimates uses more information and would provide a better estimate.

3 A member of the population chosen at random has probability p of being a Conservative voter. Since the population is very large, this probability is (virtually) the same for each member of the sample independently of the voting intention of other members of the sample.

The distribution of X is therefore that of a binomial with 400 trials and probability of success p.

4 Part of inequality 1 is:

$$400p - 1.96\sqrt{400p(1-p)} < X$$
$$\Rightarrow 400p < X + 1.96\sqrt{400p(1-p)}$$
$$\Rightarrow p < \frac{X}{400} + 1.96\sqrt{\frac{p(1-p)}{400}}$$

The other half of inequality 1 is:

$$X < 400p + 1.96\sqrt{400p(1-p)}$$
$$\Rightarrow X - 1.96\sqrt{400p(1-p)} < 400p$$
$$\Rightarrow \frac{X}{400} - 1.96\sqrt{\frac{p(1-p)}{400}} < p$$

Combining the two inequalities for p gives inequality 2.

Exercise F (p. 93)

1 (a) (i) $p = 0.178$, $q = 0.822$, $n = 10\ 284$

$$0.178 - 1.96\sqrt{\frac{(0.178)(0.822)}{10\ 284}}$$
$$< p < 0.178 + 1.96\sqrt{\frac{(0.178)(0.822)}{10\ 284}}$$
$$\Rightarrow 0.171 < p < 0.185$$

i.e. between 17.1% and 18.5%

(ii) $p = 0.418$, $q = 0.582$, $n = 10\ 284$

The 95% confidence interval is (40.8%, 42.8%).

(b) $p = 0.573$, $q = 0.427$, $n = 10\ 284$

The 90% confidence interval is (56.8%, 57.8%).

(c) $p = 0.555$, $q = 0.445$, $n = 1119$

The 99% confidence interval is (51.7%, 59.3%).

(d) From (a), it can be seen that a 95% confidence interval is approximately of the form $p \pm 1\%$.

If p were rounded to the nearest 1%, this would increase the possible error to ±1.5%, which would not be sensible. Conversely, it would be unreasonable to give p to ±0.01%, given a band as wide as ±1%. To 1 d.p. therefore seems the most appropriate precision.

2 (a) (i) For males, the 95% confidence interval is

$$0.67 \pm 1.96 \sqrt{\frac{0.67 \times 0.33}{444}}$$

i.e. 0.63 to 0.71

(ii) For females, the interval is

$$0.72 \pm 1.96 \sqrt{\frac{0.72 \times 0.28}{306}}$$

i.e. 0.67 to 0.77

(b) $0.19 \pm 1.645 \sqrt{\frac{0.19 \times 0.81}{313}}$

i.e. 0.15 to 0.23

3 (a) 12 out of 30 are marked. The estimate of the proportion is $\frac{12}{30} = 0.4$.

Confidence interval:

$0.4 \pm 1.96 \sqrt{\frac{0.4 \times 0.6}{30}}$

i.e. 0.22 to 0.58.

(b) The estimated number of fish in the lake is N.

The upper limit for N is $\frac{50}{0.22} = 227$

and the lower limit for N is $\frac{50}{0.58} = 86$.

There are between 86 and 227 fish in the lake.

4 (a) Estimate of $p = 0.5$
The council requires $p \pm 0.02$.
The 90% interval for p is $p \pm 1.645$ s.e.

$1.645 \sqrt{\frac{0.5 \times 0.5}{n}} \leqslant 0.02 \Rightarrow n \geqslant 1692$

The council should select a sample of at least 1692 people.

(b) $0.02 \geqslant 1.96 \sqrt{\frac{0.5 \times 0.5}{n}} \Rightarrow n \geqslant 2401$

7 Expectation and variance

A Expected value E(x) (p. 96)

1D It depends what you mean by 'expect'. All values are equally likely.

However if the die is rolled a large number of times we would 'expect' an average score of about 3.5.

2 (a) $s(= 1, 2, ..., 6)$, $P(S = s) = \frac{1}{6}$,

expected frequency $= \frac{100}{6} = 16.7$

(b) $\frac{\sum fx}{\sum f} = \frac{350}{100} = 3.5$

(c) Also gives 3.5

(e) 3.5

(f) Always 3.5. Expected average is always 3.5 for any number of rolls.

3

t	2	3	4	5	6	7	8	9	10	11	12
$P(T=t)$	$\frac{1}{36}$	$\frac{2}{36}$	$\frac{3}{36}$	$\frac{4}{36}$	$\frac{5}{36}$	$\frac{6}{36}$	$\frac{5}{36}$	$\frac{4}{36}$	$\frac{3}{36}$	$\frac{2}{36}$	$\frac{1}{36}$
$t \times P(T=t)$	$\frac{3}{36}$	$\frac{6}{36}$	$\frac{12}{36}$	$\frac{20}{36}$	$\frac{30}{36}$	$\frac{42}{36}$	$\frac{40}{36}$	$\frac{36}{36}$	$\frac{30}{36}$	$\frac{22}{36}$	$\frac{12}{36}$

$E(T) = \sum t\,P(T=t) = 7$

Exercise A (p. 97)

1 $E(Y) = 1 \times 0.5 + 2 \times 0.25 + 3 \times 0.25 = 1.75$

2

s	1	2	3	4	5	6	8	10	12
$P(S=s)$	$\frac{1}{12}$	$\frac{2}{12}$	$\frac{1}{12}$	$\frac{2}{12}$	$\frac{1}{12}$	$\frac{2}{12}$	$\frac{1}{12}$	$\frac{1}{12}$	$\frac{1}{12}$
$s \times P(S=s)$	$\frac{1}{12}$	$\frac{4}{12}$	$\frac{3}{12}$	$\frac{8}{12}$	$\frac{5}{12}$	$\frac{12}{12}$	$\frac{8}{12}$	$\frac{10}{12}$	$\frac{12}{12}$

$E(S) = \sum s\,P(S=s) = \frac{63}{12} = 5\frac{1}{4}$

3

v	1	2	3	4	5	6	7	8	9	10
$P(V=v)$	$\frac{1}{13}$	$\frac{1}{13}$	$\frac{1}{13}$	$\frac{1}{13}$	$\frac{1}{13}$	$\frac{1}{13}$	$\frac{1}{13}$	$\frac{1}{13}$	$\frac{1}{13}$	$\frac{4}{13}$
$v \times P(V=v)$	$\frac{1}{13}$	$\frac{2}{13}$	$\frac{3}{13}$	$\frac{4}{13}$	$\frac{5}{13}$	$\frac{6}{13}$	$\frac{7}{13}$	$\frac{8}{13}$	$\frac{9}{13}$	$\frac{40}{13}$

$E(V) = \frac{85}{13} = 6\frac{7}{13}$

4 $p = 0.03$ (as total probability is 1) and
$E(X) = 0 + 0.1 + 0.4 + 0.21 + 0.12 = 0.83$

B Expectation of a function of a random variable (p. 98)

1

s	$p = 2s$	$P(P=p)$	$p \times P(P=p)$
1	2	$\frac{1}{6}$	$\frac{2}{6}$
2	4	$\frac{1}{6}$	$\frac{4}{6}$
3	6	$\frac{1}{6}$	$\frac{6}{6}$
4	8	$\frac{1}{6}$	$\frac{8}{6}$
5	10	$\frac{1}{6}$	$\frac{10}{6}$
6	12	$\frac{1}{6}$	$\frac{12}{6}$

$E(P) = \sum pP(P=p) = 7$

2 Similarly $E(R) = 10$

3 $R = 2S + 3$, $E(R) = 2 \times E(S) + 3$

4 (a) $E(aX) = aE(X)$
(b) $E(X + b) = E(X) + b$
(c) $E(aX + b) = aE(X) + b$

5E (a)

s^2	$P(S^2 = s^2)$	$s^2 \times P(S^2 = s^2)$
1	$\frac{1}{6}$	$\frac{1}{6}$
4	$\frac{1}{6}$	$\frac{4}{6}$
9	$\frac{1}{6}$	$\frac{9}{6}$
16	$\frac{1}{6}$	$\frac{16}{6}$
25	$\frac{1}{6}$	$\frac{25}{6}$
36	$\frac{1}{6}$	$\frac{36}{6}$
	1	$\frac{91}{6}$

$E(S^2) = \frac{91}{6} = 15\frac{1}{6}$

(b) (i) $17\frac{1}{6}$ (ii) $18\frac{2}{3}$ (iii) $\frac{441}{6} = 73\frac{1}{2}$

6 fs^2 values: 16.7, 66.7, 150, 266.7, 416.7, 600
So $\sum fs^2 = 1516.8$
So 'expected variance'
$V(S) = \frac{1516.8}{100} - 3.5^2 \approx 2.92$

7 $s^2 \times P(S^2 = s^2)$ values: $\frac{1}{6}, \frac{4}{6}, \frac{9}{6}, \frac{16}{6}, \frac{25}{6}, \frac{36}{6}$
So $\sum s^2 \times P(S^2 = s^2) = \frac{91}{6}$
So $V(S) = \frac{91}{6} - 3.5^2 \approx 2.92$ as in question 6.

8

x	$P(X=x)$	$x\,P(X=x)$	$x^2\,P(X=x)$
0	$\frac{1}{32}$	0	0
1	$\frac{5}{32}$	$\frac{5}{32}$	$\frac{5}{32}$
2	$\frac{10}{32}$	$\frac{20}{32}$	$\frac{40}{32}$
3	$\frac{10}{32}$	$\frac{30}{32}$	$\frac{90}{32}$
4	$\frac{5}{32}$	$\frac{20}{32}$	$\frac{80}{32}$
5	$\frac{1}{32}$	$\frac{5}{32}$	$\frac{25}{32}$
	1	$\frac{80}{32}$	$\frac{240}{32}$

$E(X) = \sum x\,P(X=x) = \frac{80}{32} = 2.5$
$E(X^2) = \sum x^2\,P(X=x) = \frac{240}{32} = 7.5$
$V(X) = E(X^2) - (E(X))^2 = 7.5 - 2.5^2 = 1.25$

9D $V(aX) = E((aX)^2) - (E(aX))^2$
$= E(a^2 X^2) - (aE(X))^2$
$= a^2 E(X^2) - a^2(E(X))^2$
$= a^2[E(X^2) - (E(X))^2] = a^2 V(X)$

$V(aX + b) = E[(aX + b)^2] - [E(aX + b)]^2$
$= E[a^2 X^2 + 2abX + b^2]$
$\quad - [aE(X) + b]^2$
$= a^2 E(X^2) + 2abE(X) + b^2$
$\quad - a^2(E(X))^2 - 2abE(X) - b^2$
$= a^2 E(X^2) - a^2(E(X))^2$
$= a^2[E(X^2) - (E(X))^2] = a^2 V(X)$

10D Various activities involving rolling dice are possible.

For example:

$X =$ score on die
$Y =$ 'score' on coin (0 for tails, 1 for heads)
$a = 2, b = 3$

Roll die and double ⎫ Now add to investigate
Toss coin and treble ⎭ $2X + 3Y$.

11 $E[X] = 0 \times q + 1 \times p = p$

$V[X] = E[X^2] - (E[X])^2$

$\qquad = 0^2 \times q + 1^2 \times p - p^2$

$\qquad = p - p^2$

$\qquad = p(1 - p)$

$\qquad = pq$

12 $E[X + Y] = E[X] + E[Y]$

So $E[X_1 + X_2 + \cdots + X_n] = E[X_1]$

$\qquad\qquad\qquad\qquad + E[X_2] + \cdots + E[X_n]$

$E[X_2] = E[X]$ for all values of i from 1 to n

Exercise B (p. 101)

1 (a) $E(Y) = 2$, $V(Y) = 1\frac{1}{3}$ (for method see question 8 on p. 128)

(b) $E(2Y) = 4$, $V(2Y) = 5\frac{1}{3}$

2

s	$P(S = s)$	$s\,P(S = s)$	$s^2\,P(S = s)$
0	0.5	0	0
1	0.2	0.2	0.2
2	0.2	0.4	1.6
3	0.1	0.3	2.7
	1	0.9	4.5

(a) $P(S = 3) = 0.1$

(b) $E(S) = 0.9$

$\qquad V(S) = 4.5 - 0.9^2 = 3.69$

(c) $E(3S) = 3 \times 0.9 = 2.7$

$\qquad V(3S) = 9 \times 3.69 = 33.21$

3 See table for question 1 on p. 128.

$E(T) = 7$

$t^2\,P(T = t)$: $\frac{4}{36}$, $\frac{18}{36}$, $\frac{48}{36}$, $\frac{100}{36}$, $\frac{180}{36}$, $\frac{294}{36}$, $\frac{320}{36}$, $\frac{324}{36}$, $\frac{300}{36}$, $\frac{242}{36}$, $\frac{144}{36}$

$E(T^2) = 54.83$

$V(T) = 54.83 - 7^2 = 5.83$

This is not the same as doubling.

For example, T can take value 7 but a double score cannot.